P9-AZX-801

A LOSS
OF MASTERY

Puritan Historians in Colonial America

JEFFERSON MEMORIAL LECTURES

A Loss
of Mastery

Puritan Historians in Colonial America

By PETER GAY

University of California Press

BERKELEY AND LOS ANGELES

UNIVERSITY OF CALIFORNIA PRESS
BERKELEY AND LOS ANGELES, CALIFORNIA

CAMBRIDGE UNIVERSITY PRESS
LONDON, ENGLAND

LIBRARY OF CONGRESS CATALOG CARD NUMBER: 67-10969
PRINTED IN THE UNITED STATES OF AMERICA

To the many thousands of pilgrims, Jewish and not Jewish, German and Austrian and Polish, whom Hitler compelled to discover America—to the memory of my father who never made a good living here but so passionately loved his adopted country that he could not bear to hear it criticized, to the spoiled, idle wives who supported their unemployable husbands by washing floors, making candy and selling underwear, to first-rate professors who preferred exile in second-rate American institutions to success in Nazi universities purchasable at the price of divorcing their Jewish wives, to the physicians forced to waste precious years as laboratory assistants and forced to pass humiliating examinations that they might practice their calling once again, to the prosperous lawyers and businessmen who took menial jobs and made new lives without losing, in the midst of their isolation and their suffering, their will to adapt to a new country, to the D. P.s who came out of the camps without their families and who, with the indelible numbers on their arms and their indelible memories, delighted in the open society of America and started new families, to Lore Segal who has written, here, and with matchless honesty, of what it meant to leave there, to poor Ilse whose childhood was blighted and life ruined by the Nazis and who in the end, even here, did not survive—to all of these, I, a fortunate man, dedicate this book, part of my own discovery of America, offering these few words, and this small volume, in honor of men and women who were in their own ways heroes, who are in danger of being forgotten and who deserve to be remembered.

Preface

This book is a preliminary report on a great subject: the writing of history in colonial America. I hope before long to return to it, to study those New England historians—William Hubbard, Thomas Prince, and Thomas Hutchinson—whom I have neglected in these pages, to add historians of the central colonies and Virginians like Robert Beverley, and to analyze that masterpiece of historical argumentation, the *Federalist Papers*. As a European historian—European both by birth and by specialization—I have found it delightful to explore the Puritan mind in America; I have found it equally delightful to discover the impressive historical literature that has grown up around seventeenth-century New England. It was as a European historian that I decided to speak about American historians, and, remembering that I was to speak at Berkeley, I thought it appropriate to speak about Puritan historians: what better subject to speak about there, in that city on a hill?

I am greatly obliged to Professor Mark Schorer and his committee for giving me the opportunity to spend two weeks at Berkeley as the Jefferson Memorial Lecturer for 1966. I am equally obliged to my hosts, William and Beverly Bouwsma, for making my stay a continuous pleasure. I am obliged, in addition, to friends and colleagues who criticized this manuscript. Eugene Rice was of special help in questions involving the complexities of Christian theology and Renaissance historiography; Richard and Beatrice Hofstadter, Robert and Barbara Cross, and John A. Garraty treated my invasion of their territory with that mixture of genial encouragement and alert severity that is most profitable to an author—at least to this author. Professor Thomas A. Schafer generously shared with me his unsurpassed knowledge of the Edwards notebooks; Professor Robert L. Middlekauff, of my host university, made a number of pertinent suggestions. My wife Ruth, as always, read every version of this book with affection-ate care, to my great profit.

Peter Gay

June 20, 1966
Ryegate, Vermont

Contents

*Recurrently the mind of America
falls into such isolation:
axioms brought to this country—
Puritanism, the social contract, Romanticism—
and here successfully tried out, have,
by the time the American experiment is completed,
ceased to be meaningful in Europe;
America is repeatedly left, so to speak,
with an institution on its hands.*

PERRY MILLER

A LOSS
OF MASTERY

Puritan Historians in Colonial America

Chapter One

The Struggle for
the Christian Past

I

IN THE BEGINNING God created the heaven and the earth, the light and every living creature, and man after his own image. And he saw that it was good. But soon there was trouble in paradise; the divine cosmic pattern was threatened almost as soon as it was laid down. The serpent raised his diabolical head and tempted man into disobedience, bringing into the world sin, pain, work, and death. Man was cast out from paradise, with the memory of his first high estate dimmed but never extinguished. Then Cain slew Abel his brother, and began the great warfare between the two cities, which rages still.

These traumatic early events set the pattern for all history. History was the working out of the war of Satan against the Saints, between those who forgot God for the love of self, and those who forgot self for the love of God. It was fought on many fronts: on an intimate stage in the souls of individuals, of fallen men panting for grace, in the invasion of Christian commonwealths by heathen armies, and perhaps worst of all, in the persecution of faithful by false Christians.

Philosophers of many schools tried to give reasons for this pervasive struggle, and one sect, the Manicheans, elevated the combat between light and darkness into its central principle. But their doctrine was a monotonous, incomprehensible dualism, and it was reserved to Christian theologians to lift the great struggle to the dignity of a historic drama. The war had begun in time, and by the grace of God would end in time. God had given man freedom and then, after man had abused it, sacrificed his only son to effect man's salvation: God had foretold through his inspired instruments, the Prophets, and his divine book, the Scriptures, that there would be a final moment when history would be taken up into eternity, and the destiny of man fulfilled. And God had hinted at his design by other means: he had chosen, from time to time, an elect nation to testify to his Word and live in his way; and, on great occasions, he had revealed himself directly, miraculously, to his astonished children. That is why the reverent study of the past—the study of Scriptures, of the Church Fathers, and of all history in the light of Christian doctrine—came to be a pursuit as pious and as important as the prayer and the self-questioning that led sinners to conversion: it taught that God cared for his creation and his creatures. Men came to understand the meaning of their lives, their place and purpose, by understanding the meaning of history, and the activity of God dictated the tasks of the historian: to discover in the myriad details of history the grand divine design, to celebrate historic moments—the sacrifice of Isaac, or the Resurrection of Christ—and to bear witness to special providential intervention in the lives of ordinary men.

For some centuries, while the memory of the Savior's mission on earth was still bright and the Christian church still truly primitive, theologians clearly discerned and honestly reported the divine program. But then came centuries of decay and betrayal and devilish innovation: Anti-Christ seized power in Rome and, once in power, arrogated authority that belonged to others, preached doctrine first enunciated by Satan. There was nothing surprising in this turn of events: it was a reenactment of Cain's hollow victory over his brother. "Since the world's beginning," John Bale wrote in 1543, iniquity has taken its perverse course, and will continue to take it "to the latter end thereof. In the very angels and spirits of heaven did God find an untoward stubbornness and an obstinate crookedness. What he hath had in the ungodly children of men since the days of Cain till this present age, it were much to write. Of that [which] was sometime the Church of Christ hath it made the synagogue of Satan ever since that adversary was set at large after the thousand years and somewhat afore, whose malignant members under the title of spirituality are always filthy whoremongers, murtherers, thieves, raverners, idolators, liars, dogs, swine, wolves, abominable workers, adversaries to God and devils incarnate."[1] It was all part of the Christian pilgrimage: the book of Revelation had foretold hail and fire, blood and pestilence, the rule of wicked Babylon, the city of fornication—and the book of Revelation was authoritative. But it had also foretold that the whore of Babylon would be overthrown, quite cast down, and that the saints would triumph. And now, after centuries of popish darkness, the light of the gospel was beginning to shine once again. Satan in his death throes continued to claim his victims, and the restoration of true belief and primitive worship was hard, painful work, but the dominant theme of recent history was recovery, the mood of historians, expectancy.

As Satan was beaten back, more and more true believers gave witness to the war between the two cities. Honest John Huss was betrayed by popish politicians and burned at the stake, and in his century and the next, many shared his glorious martyr's fate, in many cities. But while the Reformation was cosmopolitan work, that work began first, and was done best, in England, to England's eternal honor. England was divinely equipped for this mission: it had been the first country beyond the immediate empire of Christ to enjoy Christianity. "Britain received the gospel in the time of Tiberius the emperor, under whom Christ suffered"—thus said St. Gildas in the sixth century;

---

[1] *Yet a Course at the Romyshe Foxe*, quoted in William Haller, *The Elect Nation: The Meaning and Relevance of Foxe's 'Book of Martyrs'* (1963), pp. 68-69.

thus said John Bale in the sixteenth century; and after John Bale, John Foxe; and after John Foxe, every Englishman who had not perversely clung to the Church of Rome.[2] Popish propagandists asserted that Christianity had come from Rome through the mission of St. Augustine of Canterbury, but that was a devilish invention like all their other inventions: Augustine had only corrupted the pure eastern Christian rites he had found. And, like its establishment, the reestablishment of Christianity urgently called for historical revision. Continental reformers, though brethren in Christ, had exaggerated the contributions of German and French reformers, from pardonable pride in the necessary work; but a candid respect for historical truth compelled recognition of English primacy and pre-eminence. Chaucer had been a pioneer in baiting ecclesiastical corruption, Wyclif the first to preach a purified faith, Tyndal the most effective propagator of God's word in the vernacular. It was a special gift of Providence to allow English martyrs to be the most courageous, and the most eloquent, among the suffering servants of Christ.

The very course of English history guaranteed the English claim for privileged status: like the children of Israel (whom Englishmen admired as their spiritual ancestors even if they would not have them in their midst), the English people had erred in the wilderness and come at last into the promised land. *Regnum Angliae, regnum*

---

[2] John Foxe, *Acts and Monuments*, ed. S. R. Cattley, 8 vols. (1837), I, 306.

Dei est, was an old, and surely a true saying: the kingdom of England was palpably the kingdom of God.[3] The advent of the Tudor dynasty confirmed it. The accession of Henry VII was a near-miracle of political reconciliation and the splendid restoration of the dynasty of King Arthur; the reign of willful Henry VIII, a flawed but potent instrument of Providence, marked the decisive break with Rome; and the reign of Elizabeth I realized a new Golden Age—not in cheap metaphor, but in literal fulfillment of ancient prophecies.

In 1559, the year after the accession of Elizabeth, John Aylmer, a Marian exile preparing to come home, spoke for his fellows in the name of his country. "God," he has England say to her children, "hath brought forth in me the greatest and excellentest treasure that He hath for your comfort and all the worlds. He would that out of my womb should come that servant of Christ John Wyclif, who begat Huss, who begat Luther, who begat the truth. What greater honour could you or I have than that it pleased Christ as it were in a second birth to be born again of me among you?"[4] It was a proud rhetorical question; the great war between the two cities, after all, would end only with the end of history. It would not do to be complacent; every Christian was on active service in Christ's army, and no soldier could relax his vigilance.

---

[3] The saying is quoted by Polydore Vergil, the Humanist historian of England, in his *Anglica Historia.* See Denys Hay, *Polydore Vergil: Renaissance Historian and Man of Letters* (1952), p. 138.

[4] Haller, *Elect Nation,* pp. 87-88.

Even in defeat, Satan was a cunning, fearsome adversary, hiding Romish spies in the vestments of English clergymen, confusing pious Englishmen with subtle theological quibbles, and otherwise obstructing the pace of purification. One could never be sure. "The elder the world waxeth," John Foxe wrote in a thoughtful postscript to the last edition of *Acts and Monuments* published in his lifetime, "the longer it continueth, the nearer it hasteneth to its end, the more Satan rageth; giving still new matter of writing books and volumes."[5] But victory was certain, more certain than it had ever been before; Providence was at last declaring its intentions. Aylmer had no hesitation: "God," he wrote, "is English."[6]

This, in outline, is the conception of history that dominated Englishmen into the age of the Stuarts, and dominated the American Puritans to the time of Jonathan Edwards: a modernized, Protestant, Anglicized theology of history developed more than a thousand years before by Orosius and St. Augustine. It drew strength from its very obviousness: more convincingly, more completely

---

[5] Foxe, *Acts and Monuments*, VIII, 754.

[6] Haller, *Elect Nation*, p. 87. This expression was by no means idiosyncratic; John Lyly among others used it: "O blessed peace, oh happy Prince, O fortunate people: The lyuing God is onely the English God" (*Euphues and His England* [1580]). See William Haller, "John Foxe and the Puritan Revolution," in Richard Foster Jones and others, *The Seventeenth Century: Studies in the History of English Thought and Literature from Bacon to Pope* (1951), p. 209.

than any rival scheme of explanation, it clarified the religious experience and organized the historical knowledge of Christian Englishmen. It gave God his glory, man his place, events their meaning—and England its due. And it drew strength also from its essential identity with the historical thinking of Christians who rejected many of its details: Continental reformers might not agree that God was English, but they were certain that he was Protestant, and in any event, whatever his nationality, they fully accepted the traditional Christian account of his historical activities. Roman Catholics could never agree that God was Protestant, although English Catholics supposed that he was probably English,[7] but whether he was English or not, Papists insisted that this view of history was theirs: Augustine was, after all, a saint, and a great saint, of the Roman Catholic Church.

All parties were sensitive to the strategic value of the past: in an age when the appeal to history retained irresistible authority and the word "innovator" was the supreme *Schimpfwort*, Catholics treated their enemies as rootless rebels, as heretics who lacked all respect for the legitimate channels of truth, as subverters of an order established by divine decree: the rock on which Christ had built his church was, after all, in Rome. "Where was

---

[7] In 1554, Cardinal Reginald Pole told Queen Mary, her husband, and her Parliament, that England had been *"prima provinciarum quae amplexa est fidem Christi,"* and to have been chosen the first nation to embrace the faith of Christ was a historic fact which, to say the least, hinted at God's national allegiance. See Haller, *Elect Nation*, p. 19.

your church before Luther?" they asked the Protestants,[8] and this pointed rhetorical question was a historian's question, designed to cut off the Reformers from the comforts of Biblical ancestry and patristic authority. The Protestants on their side, though uncomfortably aware that their ideas seemed new and radical, also benefited from the appeal to history. Puritans assimilated the sufferings of their friends to the sufferings of early Christians, claiming for the victims of Bloody Mary, of St. Bartholomew's Day—and of Anglican harassment—the ancient honorable title of martyr. Anglicans used history against Puritans, Puritans used history against Anglicans: each found grounds in the records of the early church for, or against, episcopacy. And both used history against Rome: "God's holy gospel, the ancient bishops, and the primitive church

---

[8] Protestants faced this inconvenient question often. Early in the seventeenth century, Sir Henry Wotton "visited the church of a friendly priest in Rome to hear the vesper music. And the priest 'seeing Sir Henry stand obscurely in a corner,' sent to him a choirboy with a small piece of paper on which he had written, 'Where was your religion to be found before Luther?' And presently Sir Henry wrote underneath, 'My religion was to be found then, where yours is not to be found now, in the written word of God'" (Owen Chadwick, *From Bossuet to Newman: The Idea of Doctrinal Development* [1957], pp. 1-2). A century later, George Hickes wrote: "I know not any work an antiquary can do more serviceable to the Church than this, which will show the faith and other chief doctrines of the English-Saxon Church to be the same as ours, and perfectly answer that never ending question: 'Where was your church before Luther?'" (David C. Douglas, *English Scholars, 1660-1730*, 2nd ed. [1951], p. 19.) For documentation on the uses of the word "innovation," see below, Bibliographical Essay, pp. 130-131.

11

do make on our side," the Anglican bishop John Jewel argued, in tones to which no Puritan could object. "We have not without just cause left these men, and rather have returned to the apostles and old catholic fathers."[9] Beside this diplomatic use, the Protestant appeal to history had its domestic use: it gave heart to dissenters beset by doubts, troubled by their respect for authority or intimidated by public pressure. It was good to know that in one's prayers, one's vestments and church appointments, one was being true to the worship of the primitive fathers. Thus all participants in the fierce struggle for the Christian past testified, each in his own way, to the vitality of the traditional historical scheme. None of the polemicists asked, Are there indeed two cities at war? or, Does Providence actually superintend history? All of them asked lesser questions, questions of fact: Who is the saint, who the sinner? In whose behalf does Providence exert its efforts?

For most Englishmen after 1558, when the dismal Catholic interlude of Queen Mary had come to an end, the answers to these questions were inescapable: the Protestants are the saints and the grateful recipients of divine favor; the Papists are the innovators, the corrupters of the primitive church, rebels against the Word. Once Queen Elizabeth had proved her capacity to keep her throne, after the Marian exiles had flooded back to England, the patriotic Protestant version of Augustine's

---

[9] *Apologia Ecclesiae Anglicanae* (1562), quoted in Norman Sykes, *Old Priest and New Presbyter* (1956), p. 178.

theology of history seized the English mind. It was everywhere, or nearly everywhere: in the vigorous, plainspoken sermons of Puritan divines urging their flocks forward to more strenuous Christianity and their government to more drastic church reforms, in the elegant treatises of Anglican bishops intent on maintaining the Elizabethan establishment unchanged, in naive chronicles of the city of London and in Sir Walter Raleigh's ambitious history of the world. Edmund Spenser put it into his poems, William Shakespeare into his plays. But there was one book that expressed this historical theology more memorably than any other: John Foxe's *Acts and Monuments*, known popularly and affectionately as Foxe's Book of Martyrs.

John Foxe was a propagandist—perhaps the most effective propagandist the Protestant cause has ever had. But he was not a liar; he did not need to be. He was certain that the plain truth, the more circumstantial the better, would do Rome enough damage. He was right: there was no need to invent, to magnify heroism, concoct dying speeches, manufacture lurid incidents. Englishmen and Englishwomen, of high station and low, bishops and yeomen, the scholarly and the illiterate, had withstood hostile examination, ill treatment in prison, and burning at the stake with a wit, a fortitude, a Christian patience, which moved the critics of these "fanatics" to reluctant admiration, and supporters to tears. Foxe was credulous, it is true; he played with mystical numbers and Biblical prophecies like any medieval monk, but this only added plausibility to his history in an age addicted to number mysticism and the search for occult meanings in Scripture. He was prolix, but then he was writing for an audience that prized expansiveness and fed its imagination on detail. He was partisan, and his charity parochial, but religious warfare exacts brutal simplicities. He developed an extensive vocabulary of abuse—some of it learned from John Bale, some distinctively his own—but his readers rejoiced in his invectives. Besides, partisan and vituperative as he was, Foxe was an energetic and scrupulous researcher; he consulted local archives, interviewed eyewitnesses, rescued forgotten records. His book is a triumph of diligence, and his reports of interrogations, of suffering and endurance, carry their own guarantee of veracity. Readers of Foxe's book trusted him, and found grim entertainment there, abundant matter to feed their hatred of Rome and their patriotism. There were the prominent martyrs, every significant detail of their life and their manner of dying meticulously preserved; there were hundreds of obscure Christians who had given up their lives in defiance of Rome, for the sake of the Word. Foxe celebrated some of his martyrs with only a sentence or an epithet—a memorable dying speech, a moving farewell, or an unforgettable epitaph; he gave his readers dramatic pictures to visualize, scenes at once infuriating and elevating: on June 18, 1557, among the "seven christian and true faithful martyrs of Christ burned at Maidstone" was one "Elizabeth a blind maiden,"[10] and there were many others like her, rescued from oblivion and

---

[10] Foxe, *Acts and Monuments*, VIII, 321.

14

enlisted in a religious crusade by the rage of a historical scholar.

While the great climax of Foxe's history is the reign of Queen Mary, its beginning lay buried in the distant past. The very title page of the book proclaims the Augustinian conception of history as the combat of the two cities: God sits in his proper place, at the top, in the center, enthroned in glory and receiving the tribute of angels. Below him to his right are Protestant martyrs, lifting their eyes to heaven and piously blowing their trumpets while the flames lick around their bodies. Below them is a homely scene: a Protestant pastor preaches the Word to his flock, while the Hebrew letters that spell out the Lord's name—Jahweh—blaze down upon the congregation in blessing, like a little sun. On God's left, in contrast, are the Roman Catholics, frowned upon by damning angels, and leered at by a devilish monster; a priest is elevating the host, another lectures a crowd that is fingering its beads, while a procession winds its way in the distance. And the book itself carries out the program that the title page announces: it begins with a minutely detailed polemical essay on "The difference between the Church of Rome that now is, and the ancient Church of Rome that then was," and then launches into the ten persecutions suffered by the early Christians as prophesied in the book of Revelation, the peace of the Church after Constantine, its decay and partial restoration. As Foxe saw it, shrewdly imposing a modern national myth on ancient Christian eschatology, the history of the English church was a microcosm of the history of the world since creation.

Generations of Englishmen saw history through Foxe's eyes. Anglicans and Puritans alike loved the Book of Martyrs, memorized it, told their children stories from it; the illiterate had it read to them and absorbed its message from its heart-rending woodcuts: archbishop Cranmer at the stake, the flames high around him, heroically putting his offending hand into the fire—the hand that had signed a craven recantation; or miserable King John, kneeling before the papal legate Pandulphus and surrendering his English crown. And less than half a century after Foxe's death, Englishmen took his book, and his philosophy of history, across the Atlantic, into the American wilderness. "Mr. Fox" was an authority for William Bradford, "our English *Martyrologer*" an authority for Cotton Mather, and an authority not merely on the facts, but on the meaning, of history.[11] Foxe, the fleeing Puritans ruefully admitted, had been right: Satan continued to rage, and continued to give "still new matter of writing books and volumes." Was it not right to frustrate Satan's designs, to battle for the heavenly city in new unspoiled surroundings, and to read about martyrs rather than to share their fate?

II

While the medieval vision of history—plausible, familiar, and dramatic—had formidable authority, it was not

---

[11] William Bradford, *History of Plymouth Plantation*, ed. W. C. Ford, 2 vols. (1912), I, 7; Cotton Mather, *Diary*, ed. W. C. Ford, 2 vols. (1911-1912), I, 230.

without competitors. By the time the Puritans settled in New England, Renaissance philosophers and Renaissance historians had been assailing the medieval tradition for three centuries. Humanist historians were for the most part devout Christians: the pagan historians of the sixteenth century, Machiavelli and Guicciardini, were ominous harbingers of the future rather than exemplars of the state of historical inquiry in their time. Renaissance historians were deeply in debt to their medieval precursors, but they were no longer medieval men, and, by the time of the late Renaissance, historical writing had become an unstable compound of piety and research, moralism and realism, Christianity and classicism.

Medieval historians were for the most part credulous—Renaissance historians raised skeptical questions about the remote past. Medieval historians were subservient to theology—Renaissance historians asserted the independent dignity of their craft, allowing history such allies as philology and rhetoric, but no master: they were inordinately fond of Cicero's classic cliché that history is the witness of time, the light of truth, the life of memory, the mistress of life, the messenger of antiquity; and they wrote their histories almost as if they believed it. Medieval historians were helpless in the face of disfigured documents, inaccurate copies, and recent forgeries—Renaissance historians developed philology into a fine art, and cleaned, copied, borrowed, and stole documents to restore the past in its integrity—at least some of the time; their favorite motto, *Ad fontes!*, was a historian's motto. Medieval historians were practically all ecclesiastics—Renaissance

17

historians were often laymen: geographers, grammarians, lawyers, and statesmen, who broke the clerical monopoly. Medieval historians were dominated by sacred numbers and Biblical prophecies which together governed their periodization—Renaissance historians, though cautiously and slowly, subverted time-honored Christian schemes like the six periods or the Four Empires, and discovered their periodic divisions not in myths or mystical mathematics but in events. Medieval historians lived devoutly in the presence of Eternal Rome: as the last Empire before the Second Coming, Rome must remain alive until the end of human, historic time—Renaissance historians recognized that if the past is to be studied as the past, men must first gain distance from it: there can be no resurrection without a preceding death. Medieval historians accepted Providence as the supreme agent of historical cause— Renaissance historians substituted for Christian Providence antique pagan ideas like Fate and Fortune. Medieval historians loved the past for the sake of God—Renaissance historians developed a new cultural type, the antiquarian, who loved the past for its own sake. Medieval historians, in sum, for all their biographies, all their chronicles, all their universal histories, were in their hearts unhistorical— Renaissance historians, whether they found in history a cyclical movement, or progress, or chaos, justified the course of history by, and within, the course of history. That is why Renaissance historians, though not yet modern historians, were the fathers of modern history. Medieval ways of historical thinking were static; they had not changed since Eusebius, Orosius, and St. Augustine. Renaissance history, on the other hand, with its realistic bent, its growing irreverence, its critical methods, developed within itself a tension, an urge for continuous improvement, that made for rapid modernization.

This evolution of the historical craft was particularly marked in the half century that preceded the Puritans' discovery of America. The Renaissance rebels had found their ideals, and many of their ideas, in their glorious rediscovery of the ancients. Livy's celebration of secular civic virtue, Tacitus' penetrating analysis of motives, Polybius' comprehensive political wisdom, all served to undermine Christian historiography. But the recovery of antiquity exacted its price: more than they knew, Renaissance historians—even self-confident pagans like Machiavelli—were imprisoned by the instruments of their liberation. Then, in the age of Elizabeth I and Henri IV, a time of religious civil war and energetic state-building, a new generation of historians arose, determined to free itself from ancestor worship as its predecessors had freed themselves from superstition. Baudouin, Bodin, and La Popelinière in France, Camden, Bacon, and Selden in England, Sarpi in Venice, groping their way but certain of their purposes, modified the methods of Renaissance historiography at point after point. They rebelled against the Humanists' view of historical causation, insisting that it is man alone who makes his own fate, and that reliance on mysterious forces like Fortuna only impedes the effective investigation of the social circumstances and human qualities that make history. They rejected the Humanists' treatment of history as the sister of rhetoric

and refused to construct imaginary speeches, which they
derided as a misplaced dramatic device and an invitation
to mendacity. They questioned the Humanists' cherished
conviction that history is the supreme didactic discipline
which teaches men to love virtue and detest vice, or, at
the least, inculcates political prudence. At this point the
reformers moved cautiously: the justification of history
as the great teacher was too ancient, too powerful, and
too popular to be discarded lightly. But they demoted
the educational effects of history into an incidental, if
useful, by-product and celebrated objectivity as the highest aim of historical writing. Historians have always
praised truth as the supreme virtue and final purpose of
their craft, but the historians of the late Renaissance
consciously developed methods to make objective truth
into an operational, rather than a mere rhetorical aim. It
is significant that these historians were the first to write
the history of history, to see their craft as subject to the
ravages, and helped by the illuminations, of time.[12] The
history of history is the first step in the criticism of history: when historians discovered the evolution of history
in the past, its future evolution was only a question of
time and favorable circumstances.

These developments in historiography were as much a
response to the needs of the age as to the tensions within

---

[12] On this point see especially Donald R. Kelley, "*Historia Integra*: François Baudouin and His Conception of History," *Journal of the History of Ideas*, XXV, No. 1 (January-March, 1964),
50.

the craft. Controversy among historians aroused interest in history but beyond this, the sixteenth and seventeenth centuries needed history as few centuries before had needed it. And historians responded: historians have always been sensitive to the demands of their culture. Religious reformers, as I have said, sought the favorable verdict of history, and Roman Catholics responded in kind. Lutherans compiled the *Magdeburg Centuries*; Baronius replied with the Papist version of church history, the *Annales ecclesiastici*; Isaac Casaubon wrecked the authority of Baronius' annals by proving Baronius ignorant of Greek and Hebrew, and naively credulous of the most improbable tales. Beside all this polemical activity among clerics, lawyers consulted, or invented, historical precedents to support the claims of their clients, whether royal or aristocratic, while natural philosophers began to study the history of science more critically, less slavishly, than ever before, to find support for their novel theories. In turn, historians drew information, methods, and philosophical ideas from theologians, politicians, and scientists. By 1630, the year that William Bradford began to write *Of Plimmoth Plantation*, Arminianism in religion, Erastianism in politics, and naturalism in science, were still distinctly radical ideas, more often suppressed than accepted, but they were becoming live options for historians. The victory of modern secular historiography was still a century off: the best seventeenth-century historians were, for the most part, clerics who exploited and refined the techniques of fifteenth- and sixteenth-century scholars to glorify their God and confound rival sects.

The Benedictine Mabillon, the Jansenist Tillemont, or the Anglican George Hickes may seem strange heirs to Renaissance historiography, but the history of history, like the history of much else, is not a neat progression from one mode of thought to another. Each period accommodates and assimilates survivals and anticipations—new ideas, ideas in their prime, and ideas kept alive only by the tenacity of conservatives. As I have suggested, late-Renaissance history was a tense, uneasy mixture of medieval eschatology, rationalist piety, and classical paganism; and by 1630, the craft of history was delicately poised on the edge of modernity.

III

The Puritans experienced the climate of the Renaissance in the manner of respectable Englishmen breathing the Italian air; it both exhilarated and inhibited them. In America as much as in England, perhaps more, Puritans respected learning; those, like the Pilgrims at Plymouth, who did not have it, deferred to those who did. Ignorance, they knew, was the mother of error; to defeat ignorance was to defeat Satan himself. In 1647, the General Court of the Massachusetts Bay Colony set up reading schools because, it observed, it is *"one chief project of that old deluder, Satan, to keep men from the knowledge of the Scriptures."*[13] The leading Puritan families in New England cherished the life of the mind; they were devoted to

---

[13] Quoted in Edmund S. Morgan, *The Puritan Family: Religion and Domestic Relations in Seventeenth-Century New England*, 2nd ed. (1966), p. 88.

classical learning and sympathetic to the new science. As they were men of The Book, they were men of books: they brought books with them on the immigrant ships, imported books from Europe as soon as they had settled, circulated their precious volumes among their friends, and disposed of them in their wills. More rapidly, and more successfully, than any other group of migrants in the long history of migration, they founded a college, supported it with admirable self-sacrifice, and watched over its progress with anxious affection. In almost every way, the Puritan oligarchs were intellectually more awake, more "enlightened" than their fellow citizens whom they served and dominated. Yet all their erudition was ultimately aimed at godliness: "*After* all, (nay, *Before* all, and *Above* all)," Cotton Mather told Puritan parents in his customary emphatic style, "Tis the *Knowledge* of the *Christian Religion*, that *Parents* are to *Teach* their *Children*."[14] Harvard, it is true, was more than a Seminary: in the seventeenth century only about half of its graduates entered the ministry. But secular learning too stood under the sign of the overriding religious purpose; the Harvard graduate who became a bookseller or a fur trader was expected to be as pious, and almost as knowledgeable in Scripture, as his classmate who entered the ministry. If, in the learned climate that New England's Puritans cherished, classicism and Christianity should conflict, or wrestle for precedence, it was never Christianity, always classicism, that must yield. This at least, in a life filled with uncertainty, was certain.

---

[14] *Ibid.*, p. 90.

It was in this atmosphere, in which religious prescriptions encouraged, directed, and constricted learning, that the Puritans read and wrote their histories. The American Puritans shared the widespread interest in historical literature, and they composed their annals, their narratives of war and state-building, their striking introspective histories of their souls, almost precisely like everyone else. William Bradford's *Of Plimmoth Plantation*, Increase Mather's life of his father, Cotton Mather's *Magnalia Christi Americana*, Samuel Sewall's diary, were neither novelties in the seventeenth century, nor isolated productions; they were, one and all, familiar examples of familiar forms. Far from being radical, the Puritans' historical writings looked to the past, not merely for their subject matter—that, after all, is the proper business of history—but for their method, their style of thinking. In the writing of history, as in all liberal study, piety came first: in 1717, William Brattle, as cultivated and as cosmopolitan a pastor as New England produced, addressed a long monitory letter to his son from his death bed. "My dear Child," he urged the younger William Brattle, "be of a Catholick Spirit." But this advice implied neither a weakening of religious fervor, nor a reversal of the Puritan hierarchy of learning: "Acquaint thy Self with History," the dying man wrote, "know something of the Mathematicks, and Physick; be able to keep Accompts Merchant like in some measure; but let Divinity be thy main Study."[15]

---

[15] Clifford K. Shipton, *New England Life in the 18th Century: Representative Biographies from 'Sibley's Harvard Graduates'* (1963), p. 198, life of William Brattle.

In these words we may read the ultimate failure of Puritan historiography, and—since the writing of history is a significant cultural activity, much like the pursuit of science or the practice of poetry—the ultimate failure of the Puritan experiment in the New World. After stirring beginnings, both the course and the writing of Puritan history descended into a glacial age. Much as the American Puritans enjoyed their history, they experienced the revolutionary developments in seventeenth- and eighteenth-century historiography as victims, not as actors, let alone as pioneers. In Europe, historians were inventing new techniques, broadening their conceptions, and rushing forward into secularism; in America, Puritans continued to write history as though nothing had changed. This was the tragedy of Puritan historiography: it had no history of its own.

Chapter Two

William Bradford

Caesar in the Wilderness

I

AMERICAN PURITANS began to write history almost
as soon as they settled in the New World, but
they did not write it as Americans. The two urgent questions that have obsessed Americans at least since
the days of the Revolution—What does America mean?
and, What does it mean to be an American?—hardly
troubled them. America was a place, like any other place,
where a Christian did his duty; America was a place, unlike any other place, where the adversaries were not false
Christians, but cruel nature and cruel savages, a place
where the great work of Reformation might be completed
at last. While the Puritans might have had some doubts
how to begin, they knew precisely who they were: they
were good Protestants and loyal Englishmen.

In the search for American identity, historians have

played a strategic part, for nations, like children, discover who they are by telling what they have done. But as the Puritan historians reported the experience of their own people, it is clear that they uprooted themselves not to discover, but to protect, their identity. Their fears outran the realities, and their rhetoric outran their fears, but in the delicate inquiry into one's self and one's lot in the world, the imagination is more meaningful than reality, and the Puritans abundantly possessed the imagination of disaster. In his *Wonder-Working Providence of Sion's Saviour in New England*, published in London in 1653, Edward Johnson put the Puritan case with affecting simplicity. After the Reformation, he wrote, "England began to decline in Religion," and, "instead of purging out Popery, a farther compliance was sought not onely in vaine Idolatrous Ceremonies, but also in prophaning the Sabbath," until "the multitude of irreligious lascivious and popish affected persons spred the whole land like Grass-hoppers." And so *"the people of Christ"* that were *"Oppressed, Imprisoned and scurrilously derided,"* gathered together to ship themselves to New England.[1]

While in England it was the threat of enforced conformity that drove the Puritans to America, for the English Separatists in Holland it was the threat of assimilation. The Separatists who had settled in Amsterdam and Leyden feared the Spaniards, ready to resume the war against the rebellious Dutch Provinces after the twelve-year

---

[1] *Johnson's Wonder-Working Providence, 1628-1651*, ed. J. Franklin Jameson (1910), pp. 23-24.

truce, and they feared disarray in their small settlements with their aging leaders. But their overriding fear was that they would simply disappear as a distinctive Christian sect. "That which was more lamentable, and of all sorowes most heavie to be borne," William Bradford, who was there, later reported, "was that many of their children," both by "the great licentiousnes of youth in that countrie, and the manifold temptations of the place, were drawne away by evill examples into extravagante and dangerous courses, getting the raines off their neks, and departing from their parents." Some turned soldiers, others sailors, "and other some worse courses, tending to dissolutnes, and the danger of their soules, to the great greefe of their parents and dishonour of God. So that they saw their posteritie would be in danger to degenerate and be corrupted."[2]

There was nothing rash about the Pilgrims' decision to abandon the lovely hospitable cities that had sheltered them for more than ten years. Almost as if to discredit such charges in advance, Bradford insisted that the English Separatists decided to emigrate to America for "sun-

[2] Bradford, *Of Plymouth Plantation*, I, 55. Bradford's nephew, Nathaniel Morton, accepted this argument in his *New Englands Memoriall*, and a hundred years later Thomas Hutchinson credited Bradford's account sufficiently to copy it almost word for word: "The manners of the Dutch were too licentious for them. Their children left them; some became soldiers, and others sailors, in the Dutch service. In a few years their posterity would have been Dutch, and their church extinct" (*The History of the Colony and Province of Massachusetts-Bay*, ed. Lawrence Shaw Mayo, 3 vols. [1936], I, 3).

drie weightie and solid reasons," reasons "found by experience," and "not out of any new fangledness, or other shuch like giddie humor, by which men are oftentimes transported to their great hurt, and danger."[3] The English Puritans moved rather more expeditiously than their brethren in the United Provinces, but they too claimed that they applied the "timly remedy" of emigration only after sober reflection.[4]

However grave their decision, the Puritans were sustained in it by the conviction that their hazardous venture was an exalted mission; they took pride in their assignment to the point of self-consciousness, and spoke endlessly of their errand into the wilderness. "Wilderness," indeed, modified by "howling," "mighty," "desolate," "salvage," and other adjectives, was the Puritans' favorite metaphor; it reminded them of the grand precedent of God's chosen people fleeing from Egyptian oppression.[5] When John Winthrop, in mid-Atlantic, preached his famous sermon to his fellow-passengers on the *Arbella*, he insisted that the visibility of his little band was high.

---

[3] Bradford, *Of Plymouth Plantation*, I, 52-53.

[4] *Ibid.*, I, 52.

[5] The popularity of this metaphor did not decline. I have counted the word 94 times in Cotton Mather's *Magnalia Christi Americana*, and I am sure I have missed several uses. "Wilderness" became an all-purpose, and hence almost meaningless, metaphor, embracing the American environment, the temptation of Jesus, Luther's suffering in his exile, king David's wandering, and, above all, the children of Israel fleeing Egypt. By the time of Cotton Mather, it had also become a rather self-indulgent metaphor.

"Whatsoever wee did, or ought to have done, when wee liued in England," he exhorted his listeners, in the familiar tones of English Utopianism, "the same must wee doe, and more allsoe, where wee goe." Equipped with a special commission from God, "entered into Covenant with Him for this worke," the Puritans must walk humbly, love one another, and act as a united community, "knitt together, in this worke, as one man." Then, and only then, would the planting of *"New England"* become a model for all to imitate: "For wee must consider that we shall be as a citty upon a hill. The eies of all people are uppon us, Soe that if wee shall deale falsely with our God in this worke we haue undertaken, and so cause him to withdrawe his present help from us, wee shall be made a story and a by-word through the world."[6]

Winthrop was perfectly serious. The success or failure of his colony mattered to God and man, to Christendom in general and England in particular. England was, and long remained, home: the source of dreaded harassment, intimate memories, and sustaining approval. The settlers expressed their nostalgia for England in the form they gave their institutions, the names they gave their towns, the prayers they addressed to their God. Some of the best educated American Puritans, like Increase Mather, were happiest back home, in England; others cherished a book

---

[6] "A Modell of Christian Charity," in *Winthrop Papers*, II (1931), 282-295. As Darrett B. Rutman has pointed out (*Winthrop's Boston: Portrait of a Puritan Town, 1630-1649* [1965], p. 4n), the famous metaphor of the "citty upon a hill" is drawn from Matthew 5:14. It was freely used by others.

published in London more than a book published in Boston. The Pilgrims at Plymouth differed from the Puritans in Massachusetts Bay in their estimation of the Anglican Church: the Congregationalists were inclined to think, or to proclaim, that they were the dutiful children of an erring mother; the Separatists insisted that they had cast off the Anglican slave of Rome, reluctantly and tearfully but decisively. But all, Pilgrims and Puritans, agreed that they, like God, were English; their histories were reports to Englishmen, divine and human, wherever they might be.

II

John Winthrop delivered his lay sermon in 1630. In the same year, William Bradford, who had governed the Plymouth settlement since 1621, began to write its history. Precisely like Winthrop, Bradford was sure that the American experiment was a religious mission, prompted less by despair than by high expectations. Debating their course of action in Leyden, the Pilgrims were animated by "a great hope, and inward zeall they had of laying some good foundations (or at least to make some way therunto) for the propagating, and advancing the gospell of the kingdom of Christ in those remote parts of the world; yea, though they should be but even as stepping-stones, unto others for the performing of so great a work."[7] Bradford's *Of Plimmoth Plantation* records the

---

[7] Bradford, *Of Plymouth Plantation*, I, 55. While, as is well known, many modern historians have expressed their doubts, the Puritans were convinced that they came to America for religious

performing of the great work from the landing in 1620 to 1647. The theme is intricate, moving, and at times majestic, and Bradford rises to it in all respects; his book, unique in the ranks of Puritan historiography, is an authentic masterpiece. Its limitations are the limitations of Puritan culture, its merits are its own.

However distinctive these merits may be, *Of Plimmoth Plantation* is unmistakably in the Augustinian tradition, part of the Protestant campaign to capture the Christian past by establishing the historical credentials of the Reformation. The book is contemporary history, but, Bradford argues in his opening sentence, such history must begin with its "occasion and Indusments." Like other great events of recent times, the "roote and rise" of the Plymouth settlement lie in far-off historical crises related in the Scriptures and the writings of the Church Fathers. The deadly combat of Cain and Abel, the wanderings of the children of Israel, the Jeremiads of the Prophets, the incarnation of Christ, the sufferings and triumph of the early church—all prefigure and make sense of the work of Wyclif and Luther and Calvin, of the martyrdom of devout Christians in the bloody reign of Queen Mary, and of the Puritan errand into the American wilderness. Satan, balked by the courage and resourcefulness of English Protestants, "begane to take him to his anciente strategemes, used of old against the first

reasons, and survived there through divine help—early in the eighteenth century, Thomas Prince opens his *Chronological History of New England, In the Form of Annals* (1736) with a firm reiteration of this conviction.

Christians"; the events of modern times are mere reenactments of "the anciente times." Bradford called Socrates Scholasticus to witness that in the fourth century "the persecutions by the heathen, and the Emperours, was not greater then of the christians one against other. The Arians, and other their complices, against the orthodoxe and true christians."[8] And he called John Foxe to witness that in the sixteenth century godly Englishmen were cruelly driven into exile. Bradford aspired to be the modern Socrates Scholasticus, the seventeenth-century Foxe, testifying to the sacrifices offered up by the orthodox and true Christians of his day.

Bradford's angle of historical vision, then, was a parochial version of the Protestant theology of history, which was itself a sectarian interpretation of the reigning Christian view: the Reformation in England had been magnificent, but it remained incomplete. "It is well knowne unto the godly and judicious," Bradford opens the first chapter of his history, "how ever since the first breaking out of the lighte of the gospell, in our Honourable Nation of England (which was the first of nations, whom the Lord adorned ther with affter that grosse darknes of popery which had covered, and overspred the christian worled) what warrs, and oppossions ever since Satan hath raised, maintained, and continued against the Saincts, from time, to time, in one sorte, or other." Satan did his work, "some times by bloody death and cruell torments, other whiles Imprisonments, banishments, and other hard usages,"

---

[8] Bradford, *Of Plymouth Plantation*, I, title page; I, 1-5.

loath to see "his kingdom should go downe, the trueth prevaile; and the churches of God reverte to their anciente puritie; and recover their primative order, libertie, and bewtie."[9] For many years godly preachers, with the divine blessing upon them, exhorted their English flocks to expel from their church the remnants of "popish trash," which have "no ground in the word of God, but are relikes of that man of sine."[10] But these pastors had called upon themselves disgrace, affliction, and persecution, until at last those who "saw the evills of these things" and "whose harts the Lord had touched with heavenly zeale for his trueth" shook off "this yoake of Antichristian bondage. And as the Lords free people, joyned them selves (by a covenant of the Lord) into a church estate, in the felowship of the Gospell, to walke in all his wayes." They were ready to pay any price, "the Lord assisting them." And "that it cost them something this ensewing historie will declare."[11]

But history, even Puritan history, was not solely an accounting of divine visitations upon the righteous. The most uncompromising Calvinist knew that the Lord tempered justice with mercy—at least sometimes. History was blessedly filled with divine interventions in behalf of his servants. Fleeing into Holland, the English Separatists saw fair and wealthy cities before them, yet soon they "saw the grimme and grisly face of povertie coming upon

[9] *Ibid.*, I, 3.
[10] *Ibid.*, I, 11.
[11] *Ibid.*, I, 20-22.

them like an armed man; with whom they must bukle, and incounter, and from whom the could not flye." But they were "armed with faith, and patience against him, and all his encounters; and though they were sometimes foyled, yet by Gods assistance they prevailed, and got the victorie."[12] Crossing the Atlantic on the *Mayflower*, a "very profane" young man harried the miserable passengers, hoping, he said, "to cast halfe of them over board before they came to their jurneys end." But the Lord struck the villain with a grievous disease, and so the young man was "him selfe the first that was throwne overboard."[13] To balance this instance of divine poetic justice, the Lord rescued a pious young man, who had accidentally fallen overboard, by letting him catch hold of the topsail halyards. Once on land, the Pilgrims needed divine assistance more than ever. They had "no freinds to wellcome them, nor inns to entertaine and refresh their weatherbeaten bodys, no houses or much less townes to repaire too"; instead they confronted "savage barbarians" ready to "fill their sides full of arrows," harsh winter, and "a hidious and desolate wildernes, full of wild beasts and willd men."[14] And the Lord did not disappoint his elect. In their first encounter with the Indians, God's "spetiall providence" kept the Pilgrims from harm;[15] a little later, they found Squanto, a trustworthy Indian who served them as guide and interpreter, a "spetiall instrument sent

---

[12] *Ibid.*, I, 37.
[13] *Ibid.*, I, 149.
[14] *Ibid.*, I, 155-156.
[15] *Ibid.*, I, 171.

of God for their good beyond their expectation."[16] The Lord acted in the Pilgrims' behalf in small ways and large, sending providential letters, providential rain, providential disaster to the wicked, and providential victory to the pious: in 1637, in a memorable intervention, God helped the Plymouth settlers and their Indian allies to capture a Pequot fort: "Those that first entered found sharp resistance from the enimie, who both shott at and grapled with them; others rane into their howses, and brought out fire, and sett them on fire, which soone tooke in their matts, and standing close togeather, with the wind, all was quickly on a flame, and therby more were burnte to death then was otherwise slain; it burnte their bowstrings, and made them unservisable. Those that scaped the fire were slaine with the sword; some hewed to peeces, others rune throw with their rapiers, so as they were quickly dispatchte, and very few escaped. It was conceived they thus destroyed about ·400· at this time. It was a fearfull sight to see them thus frying in the fyer, and the streams of blood quenching the same, and horrible was the stinck and sente ther of; but the victory seemed a sweete sacrifice, and they gave the prays therof to God, who had wrought so wonderfully for them, thus to inclose their enimise in their hands, and give them so speedy a victory over so proud and insulting an enemie."[17]

Bradford knew that it was in the course of nature for

---

[16] *Ibid.*, I, 202.
[17] *Ibid.*, II, 250-252.

some men to drown and others to be rescued, for rain to fall at a propitious time and for Indians to be stupid; he was not notably credulous or superstitious, and his work is pervaded with tough-minded realism. But he did not think that nature and history were in any way autonomous realms. His providential explanations were more than pious commonplaces, more than theological circumlocutions for natural events. On this matter Bradford, his fellow historians, and hundreds of Puritan divines were clear and sure and consistent: the Lord's hand was on all things, in all history, often in tangible ways. When Puritans join in a business partnership—always a touchy affair—and loyally fulfill their obligations, Bradford is moved to see in this "rare example" of "brotherly love, and Christian care," something "more then of man": such conduct must be "the spetiall worke and hand of God."[18] Again, when the leaders of the Pilgrims, like their revered Elder, William Brewster, live to sixty or more, some even to "nere ·80·," surviving "chaing of aeir, famine, or unholsome foode, much drinking of water, sorrows and troubles," all of these "enimies to health, causes of many diseaces, consumers of naturall vigoure and the bodys of men, and shortners of life," then this too "must needs be more then ordinarie, and above naturall reason." And so Bradford takes time "not only to mention" these things, "but greatly to admire the marvelous providence of God."[19] The very survival of the New

---

[18] *Ibid.*, II, 68.
[19] *Ibid.*, II, 351.

England enterprise had "more then of man" behind it: "Thus out of smalle beginnings greater things have been produced by his hand that made all things of nothing, and gives being to all things that are; and as one small candle may light a thousand, so the light here kindled hath shone to many, yea in some sorte to our whole nation; let the glorious name of Jehova have all the praise."[20] There can be no doubt: when Bradford set it down that "Man m[a]y purpose, but God doth dispose,"[21] he was making a sober statement of fact.

III

William Bradford testified to his Puritan faith in simple words and homely metaphors, but he was in his own way a learned man. It would be fatuous to portray him as an erudite pedant poring over the latest treatises on the art of history. He was the son of a yeoman, and largely self-educated; during his years of exile in Amsterdam and Leyden, he made his living as a weaver. But he had the Puritans' thirst for learning. "He was a Person for *Study* as well as *Action*," Cotton Mather said of him, and added, with justified pride and only moderate over-statement: "He attained unto a notable Skill in *Language*; the *Dutch* Tongue was become almost as Vernacular to him as the *English*; the *French* Tongue he could also manage; the *Latin* and the *Greek* he had Mastered; but the

---

[20] *Ibid.*, II, 117.
[21] *Ibid.*, I, 444.

Hebrew he most of all studied."[22] Bradford in fact read widely, constantly, and purposefully: he read the Geneva Bible, and its accents reverberate through his history; he read technical treatises on church organization, Protestant apologetics and hagiography; and he read history, including "The Guiciardin," Eusebius' history of the early church, Vives' edition of Augustine's *City of God*, and, of course, Foxe's Book of Martyrs.[23] His interpretation of history may have been parochial, but his knowledge of it was comprehensive: *Of Plimmoth Plantation* is at a level of information, analysis, and style that can compete in all respects with John Winthrop's journal—and Winthrop was a gentleman who had attended Cambridge.

Like any Puritan of the heroic age, Bradford had only scorn for ostentatious erudition; he acquired his knowledge for the sake, and tested it in the course, of religious controversy. As a young man, it seems, he was compelled to defend his fervent Separatist convictions against the ridicule of his neighbors and the disapproval of his family.[24] In his Dutch exile, he witnessed the acrimonious but instructive debates between Dutch Arminians and Dutch Calvinists, debates in which the most articulate of the English Separatists participated on the side of ortho-

[22] *Magnalia Christi Americana*, ed. Thomas Robbins, 2 vols. (1853-1855), I, 113 (in "Galeacius Secundus. The Life of William Bradford, Esq., Governour of Plymouth Colony").

[23] See Thomas Goddard Wright, *Literary Culture in Early New England, 1620-1730* (1920), p. 27.

[24] Here we must rely on Cotton Mather's biography; see *Magnalia Christi Americana*, I, 110.

doxy; as governor of Plymouth for thirty years, he was repeatedly embroiled in theological polemics, refuting Anglicans, rebuking Antinomians, reviling papists. But not all of Bradford's reading was narrowly utilitarian. Late in life, he set himself to study the language of God. "Though I am growne aged," he wrote, as a preface to his Hebrew exercises, "yet I have had a longing desire to see, with my owne eyes, somthing of that most ancient language, and holy tongue, in which the Law and Oracles of God were write; and in which God and angels spake to the holy patriarks of old time; and what names were given to things from the creation. And though I cañot attaine to much herein, yet I am refreshed to have seen some glipse hereof; (as Moyses saw the land of Canan a farr of.) My aime and desire is, to see how the words and phrases lye in the holy texte; and to discerne somewhat of the same, for my owne contente."[25]

Here, in this private gesture, William Bradford the Puritan stands before posterity at his most characteristic and his most appealing. His piety is fundamentalist: Bradford credits the literal meaning of the Biblical narrative. It is aesthetic and personal: submissive as he is, Bradford is intently curious to discover "how the words and phrases lye in the holy texte," with his "owne eyes" and for his "owne contente." *Of Plimmoth Plantation* was written with the same piety, from the same impulse.

Bradford's history therefore offers few surprises. Its piety makes it Puritan; its sense of special election makes it English; its general contours—the annalistic mode, its

---

[25] Massachusetts Historical Society, *Proceedings*, XI (October, 1870), 402.

use of extensive quotations—are typical of most histories then in circulation.[26] But Bradford's book is not simply representative of English Puritanism; Bradford's American situation both dictated his theme and restricted his range. Sir Walter Raleigh, living as he did in a wider world, could attempt to write universal history; William Camden, commanding as he did a larger past, could write a comprehensive history of England. Bradford protectively, fiercely, concentrated on his chosen handful of pilgrims. They were his family, his flock, his life, and they engrossed his history. "And the time being come that they must departe," Bradford wrote in a famous paragraph, describing the Pilgrims' farewell to Holland, "they were accompanied with most of their brethren out of the citie, unto a towne sundrie miles of called Delfes-Haven, wher the ship lay ready to receive them. So they lefte the goodly and pleasante citie, which had been ther resting place near · 12 · years; but they knew they were pilgrimes, and looked not much on those things, but lift up their eyes to the heavens, their dearest cuntrie, and quieted their spirits. When they came to the place they found the ship and all things ready; and shuch of their freinds as could not come with them followed after them, and sundrie also came from Amsterdame to see them shipte and to take their leave of them. That night was spent with litle sleepe by the most, but with freindly entertainmente and christian discourse and other reall

---

[26] Strictly speaking, *Of Plimmoth Plantation* does not begin as annals. Book I ends with the landing of the Pilgrims; then Bradford notes that "the rest of this history (if God give me life, and opportunitie) I shall, for brevitis sake, handle by way of annalls" (I, 187).

expressions of true christian love. The next day, the wind being faire, they went aborde, and their freinds with them, where truly dolfull was the sight of that sad and mournfull parting; to see what sighs and sobbs and praires did sound amongst them, what tears did gush from every eye, and pithy speeches peirst each harte; that sundry of the Dutch strangers that stood on the key as spectators, could not refraine from tears. Yet comfortable and sweete it was to see shuch lively and true expressions of dear and unfained love. But the tide (which stays for no man) caling them away that were thus loath to departe, their Reve[ren]d pastor falling downe on his knees, (and they all with him,) with watrie cheeks commended them with most fervente praiers to the Lord and his blessing. And then with mutuall imbrases and many tears, they tooke their leaves one of an other; which proved to be the last leave to many of them."[27] This passage is everything it has been called: Biblical and moving and beautiful, but above all, it embodies a loyalty, solidarity, pride in a tribe and identification with its fate, that leaves little room for outsiders. *Of Plimmoth Plantation* is a miniature in an enormous frame: the outside world existed for Bradford, but only as a supporter, a Satanic enemy, a weeping sympathetic spectator; the distant past existed for him, but only as it prefigured the historic mission of his Pilgrims.

Inescapably, such intense concentration of attention made Bradford a contemporary historian. It was a risky and, at least to some historians, a questionable enterprise;

---

[27] Bradford, *Of Plymouth Plantation*, I, 121-125.

while such respected historians as Guicciardini and de
Thou had chronicled the events of their own day, Bradford's contemporaries still cited the old Humanist decree
that the historian who has participated in the events he
describes is less dignified than the historian who must
construct his book from documents. In 1614, while Bradford was still living at Leyden, Sir Walter Raleigh, whom
Bradford and other Puritans much admired, had warned
against contemporary history: "I know that it will bee
said by many, that I might have beene more pleasing to
the Reader, if I had written the Story of mine owne
times; having been permitted to draw water as neare the
Well-head as another. To this I answer, that who-so-ever
in writing a modern Historie, shall follow truth too neare
the heeles, it may happily strike out his teeth. There is no
Mistresse or Guide, that hath led her followers and servants into greater miseries."[28] Raleigh agreed with the
Italian Humanists that Caesar, for all his literary gifts, was
less worthy of imitation than Livy or Sallust.

But Bradford had no choice. He was a Caesar, and
while to write Caesar's kind of history might reduce his
chances for lasting fame, it offered him opportunities
denied to others. Like Caesar, Bradford had witnessed
stirring events, and witnessed them more closely perhaps
than anyone else; like Caesar, Bradford had had a decisive
voice in the shaping of these events; like Caesar, Bradford
had the urge and the talent to record what he had seen
and done. Two difficulties—it is often argued—beset, or

---

[28] *The History of the World*, Preface, near the end.

vitiate, the writing of contemporary history: the lack of documents and the pressure of prejudice. The first of these never troubled Bradford at all. As a prominent man of action, he had ready access to the materials he needed, and he preserved them in his letter book or in the official records. As governor, he made the documents which, as historian, he later quoted.

Prejudice was another matter. It is hardly necessary to insist that Bradford was committed to his holy experiment and that, as one of its leaders, he made policy which he thought to be—and because he thought it to be—right. He did not write his history as an apology, nor did he need to: he had little to apologize for. But his historical vision was the vision of a partisan. Bradford was never dishonest, or sly, or disingenuous; he was simply sure that his opponents were wrong: that is why they were his opponents.

One such opponent was the preacher John Lyford, a nuisance to the Plymouth settlement who goaded Bradford into one of his rare outbursts of sarcasm. When Lyford first came to Plymouth, "he saluted" the settlers "with that reverence and humilitie as is seldome to be seen, and indeed made them ashamed, he so bowed and cringed unto them, and would have kissed their hands if they would had suffered him; yea, he wept and shed many tears, blessing God that had brought him to see their faces; and admiring the things they had done in their wants, etc. as if he had been made all of love, and the humblest person in the world. And all the while (if we may judg by his after cariages) he was but like him mentioned in Psa. 10. 10. That crouchetch and boweth, that heaps of poore may fall by his might."[29] Once settled, Lyford gathered a turbulent faction and sent letters to England slandering the Pilgrims and plotting their ruin. But the government intercepted these letters and opened them, and, after dramatic confrontations and patient waiting for a reformation that never came, expelled him.

This, with much circumstantial and plausible detail, is Bradford's account of Lyford's character and activities. It is amusing and devastating—more than one later historian has read it as an anticipation of Dickens' portrait of Uriah Heep.[30] But is it wholly trustworthy? By his own confession, Lyford was a stubborn, troubled, sensual man, restless, aimless, unable to tolerate the tedium of a regular

---

[29] Bradford, *Of Plymouth Plantation*, I, 380-381.

[30] Thus Moses Coit Tyler: Lyford was a "Uriah Heep," a "mischievous clerical impostor" and a "fawning swindler" (*A History of American Literature, 1607-1765* [1878; reprinted 1962], p. 128); James Truslow Adams: Lyford was a "canting hypocritical clergyman," a "sort of lascivious Uriah Heep" (*The Founding of New England* [1921], pp. 106-107); Kenneth B. Murdock: Lyford is presented as a "Uriah Heep," and in Bradford's description, irony is "keyed to accurate characterization" (*Literature and Theology in Colonial New England* [1949], p. 82). See also Samuel Eliot Morison's contemptuous comment on Lyford in his edition of *Plymouth Plantation* (p. 148n). There is nothing untoward in these repetitions; any literate reader of Bradford's characterization must inevitably think of Dickens' immortal villain. But how can all these historians be so sure? They have simply taken Bradford's word, and Bradford was witness, prosecutor, and judge. The single exception is Charles M. Andrews; see his skeptical observations on the Lyford incident in his *The Colonial Period of American History*, I (1934), 267-277.

life. Doubtless, such a man was a real nuisance, and Bradford speaks of him with indignation and contempt. But other nuisances were suffered to remain; Lyford was an intolerable threat because he was an uncomfortable reminder. Whether he was regularly ordained or not, Lyford was an Anglican, and his clerical activities warned his Puritan masters that their hold on the settlement was rather more precarious than they liked to think. "We have rid ourselves of the company of many of those, who have been so troublesome to us," Bradford wrote to Robert Cushman at Leyden on June 9, 1625, not long after Lyford and his friends had been driven out, "though I fear we are not yet rid of the troubles themselves."[31] Those troubles—Anglicans and other settlers, doubtless a sizable group, who thought that the Puritans' religiosity was a little excessive—do not find a sympathetic hearing in Bradford's history.

Yet the partisanship of *Plimmoth Plantation* is far from apparent. Bradford makes his case persuasive—that is, he makes it sound not like a case, but like history—by a device that historians of contemporary events have employed since Thucydides: modesty. Bradford's skill at keeping himself out of his book has often been noted; it takes some effort to discover him in occasional references to "the governor." This modesty gives Bradford's narrative an air of inevitability; it is not Bradford who speaks, Bradford who decides, Bradford who voices his likes and

---

[31] *Governour Bradford's Letter Book, Collections of the Massachusetts Historical Society*, first series, III (1794), 36.

dislikes—it is history itself that addresses the reader through the passive, accurate, self-effacing narrator. And Bradford's self-effacement only gains in power by being sometimes set aside. There are moments, rare moments, when Bradford chooses to speak in his own voice, and then he speaks with compelling authority. Thomas Morton of Merrymount, a greater nuisance to the Pilgrims even than Lyford, had been conducting drunken parties, selling guns to the Indians, and, it seems, telling them how to make gunpowder: "O the horiblenes of this vilanie! how many both Dutch and English have been latly slaine by those Indeans, thus furnished. . . . Oh! that princes and parlaments would take some timly order to prevente this mischeefe, and at length to suppress it, by some exemplerie punishmente upon some of these gaine thirsthie murderers (for they deserve no better title,) before their collonies in these parts be over throwne by these barbarous savages, thus armed with their owne weapons, by these evill instruments, and traytors to their neigbors and cuntrie. But"—and the wrathful Jeremiah hastens to leave the stage—"I have forgott my selfe, and have been to longe in this digression; but now to returne."[32] Who, after this, would dare to rescue Morton's reputation, to retouch this portrait?

IV

For all this reticence, *Of Plimmoth Plantation* is a deeply personal book; William Bradford speaks in his own

---

[32] Bradford, *Of Plymouth Plantation*, II, 53-54.

voice. That voice, to be sure, reverberates with echoes. The "plain stile," which, Bradford tells his readers, is to be the style of his history, makes *Of Plimmoth Plantation* a Protestant book. More than the Roman Catholics, the Reformers aimed at vigor, directness, sonority, emphasis; seeking a wide audience for God's word, they constructed forms of discourse designed to be "understanded of the people."[33] And the Puritans made these aims peculiarly their own. While Anglican Priests indulged in elegant constructions, scholarly allusions, and metaphysical wit, the Puritans had only aversion for the "airy dews of effeminate rhetoric."[34] In America, especially, preachers called for, and delivered, sermons in "homely dresse and course habit," suitable to *the wildernesse,* where curiosity is not studied."[35] Bradford was fortunate; he lived in a great age of the English language.

But environment is never an adequate explanation for the triumphs of talent. Many Puritan writers were heavy-handed, dull, commonplace. Bradford was a born writer, with an exquisite ear and superb taste. His style was plain, but not unrelieved; he skillfully varied, and thus em-

---

[33] Bradford advertises his "plain stile" on the title page. The demand that sermons be "understanded of the people" is contained in the *Book of Common Prayer*, in the article, "Of Speaking in the Congregation."

[34] Dr. Samuel Crook, an English parson, quoted in H. C. Porter, *Reformation and Reaction in Tudor Cambridge* (1958), p. 226.

[35] Thomas Hooker, *Survey of the Summe of Church-Discipline* (1648), quoted in Perry Miller and Thomas H. Johnson, eds., *The Puritans*, 2 vols., rev. ed. (1963), II, 672-673.

phasized, the majestic course of his narrative with playful devices drawn from the ornate writing of his day: lyrical descriptions, extended metaphors, alliterative phrases, and balanced sentences. These devices were available to all; what is striking is Bradford's tactful management of the resources at his command. His occasional use of wit or ornament does not deflect him from his purpose. The metaphors which make *Of Plimmoth Plantation* so memorable are never mere brilliant decorations designed to display the historian's erudition or literary skill. They owe their existence, and in turn lend energy, to Bradford's material. The young Pilgrims in Holland, drawn away from their parents by evil examples, get "the raines of their neks," while in their turn godly Englishmen, restless under Anglican harassment, shake "of this yoake." Poverty is like "an armed man," with a "grimme and grisly face." Here are pictures, natural, unaffected, economical, artless—and artful—to be understood of the people.

This is not all. Style, especially a style like Bradford's, does not subsist in isolation; manner has matter behind it. With Bradford this matter is sadness, his most intimate and most poignant quality. Sadness is not depression, but in the course of Bradford's life, and particularly in the twenty years it took him to write his history, his customary gravity deepened into melancholy. It should not be necessary to refute once again the durable caricature of the dour Puritan: in England as in America, the Puritans laughed, drank wine, wrote poetry, enjoyed verbal play and colorful dress—in moderation—and took so much pleasure in lawful sexual intercourse that none of them remained a widow, or a widower, for long. But the Puritan was driven by a high purpose, and as he made strong demands on himself, his sense of guilt was well developed, his fear of failure acute. As the American Utopia grew into a settlement, the errand into an institution, the first generation of settlers became nostalgic for the old fervor, the heroic spirit of the early years, and solemnly warned against Satan's new stratagems.

Of Plimmoth Plantation reflects this nostalgia and this fear. The finest, certainly the most famous, scenes in the book depict an arrival; but the last scenes depict departures. After so much suffering, so much hard work, so much argument with greedy merchant adventurers and unscrupulous colonial agents, the little family at Plymouth seems ready to scatter. Bradford was obsessed with this theme: the poems he wrote in his last years dwell, in limping amateurish couplets, on decay and loss. After years in a howling wilderness, after famine and Indian wars, the Pilgrims had, with God's help, built a sturdy town and laid out flourishing farms, imported godly ministers, and appointed prudent magistrates. But then,

> I am loath (indeed) to change my theme,
> Thus of God's precious mercies unto them;
> Yet must I do it, though it is most sad,
> And if it prove otherwise, I shall be glad.
> Methinks I see some great change at hand,
> That ere long will fall upon this poor land;
> Not only because many are took away,
> Of the best rank, but virtue doth decay,

And true godliness doth not now so shine,
As some whiles it did, in the former time.

Christian love and Christian zeal are going to sleep, while "security and the world on men do creep"; with wealth and power have come pride and oppression and religious error, but worst of all, covetousness and irreligion. The pure commonwealth has been invaded by sinners:

Another cause of our declining here,
Is a *mixt multitude*, as doth appear.
Many for servants hither were brought,
Others came for gain, or worse ends they sought.

In the 1650's, as Bradford wrote these and similar lines, his haven had become unrecognizable.[36]

Of Plimmoth Plantation chants the same litany, and, since Bradford was not much of a poet, to greater effect. Only twenty years after the Pilgrims had settled, Bradford observes, "wickednes did grow and breake forth," in the very sacred place to which God had sent his servants to serve him with special zeal. Perhaps, Bradford suggests, it is because Satan, envious of God's might, is especially active in such a place; perhaps it is because wickedness is most prominent in a Christian settlement where goodly men are zealous in uncovering it; perhaps it is because in a colony where men are scarce, wicked-

---

[36] *Governour Bradford's Letter Book*, 81. The "mixt multitude," of course, recalls the exodus from Egypt (see Exodus 12:38). There had been intimations earlier than this that the holy community was less than holy—as early as the 1630's, as Bradford acknowledges, his experiment in pious communism had failed.

ness is most visible: "horrible evills" are "as it were, brought into the light, and set in the plaine feeld, or rather on a hill, made conspicuous to the veiw of all."[37] Thus John Winthrop's glowing Biblical metaphor has become a vehicle for disheartened speculation.

But whatever the causes might be, Bradford found declension palpable and terrifying. It was marked by the rise of religious dissension, the appearance of sectarian aberration, the outbreak of violence, and the growing incidence of sexual uncleanness, including the dreadful case of young Thomas Granger, detected, convicted, and executed for "buggery" with "a mare, two goats, five sheep, ·2· calves, and a turkey."[38] But worst of all, some of Plymouth's finest citizens were leaving to settle elsewhere: "And thus was this poore church left, like an anciente mother, growne olde, and forsaken of her children, (though not in their affections,) yett in regarde of their bodily presence and personall helpfullnes. Her anciente members being most of them worne away by deathe; and these of later time being like children translated into other families, and she like a widow left only to trust in God. Thus she that had made many rich became her selfe poore."[39] Bradford's annals turn at the end into elegy. On the last page of the manuscript, there is this entry: "Anno 1647. And Anno 1648." Nothing else. And so, Bradford ends his history in silence.

---

[37] Bradford, *Of Plymouth Plantation*, II, 308-310.

[38] *Ibid.*, II, 328. Ironically, this was another legacy from England: the Plymouth Sodomites confessed that they had "long used it in old England" (*Ibid.*, II, 329).

[39] *Ibid.*, II, 369.

Chapter Three

Cotton Mather

A Pathetic Plutarch

I

THE FOUNDING FATHERS of New England had written their histories under the pressure of great events, with all the passionate immediacy of the participant. But by the 1660's, their day was over. William Bradford died in 1657; Edward Winslow had preceded him by two years, John Winthrop by eight. Edward Johnson lived on to 1672, but after publishing his *Wonder-Working Providence of Sions Saviour in New England*—that naive military bulletin reporting Christ's victories against Satan in America—he allowed his official duties to engross his time, and wrote no more.

They had all been devout chroniclers, looking up to heaven as their dearest country, but significantly they had all been laymen, public servants who composed their an-

nals from a fund of political experience. The generation
of historians that took their place were all clerics. They
were scarcely less active in public affairs than the statesmen who had preceded them, and no more fanatical, but
as the appointed guardians of the Puritan conscience, they
turned the writing of history into a self-conscious pursuit. Intermittent warfare with the Indians in the 1670's
and 1680's produced some splendidly artless chronicles,
narratives alive with terror and the pious thirst for blood,
but for the most part the production of history became a
tribal rite, almost a religious act.

The historians of the second generation drew heavily
on the first for their documentation, their standards of
excellence, their mode of historical thinking. Their deriv-
ative mentality was not wholly regrettable; what they
lost in originality, they gained in professional piety for
the work of the Founders, notably for Bradford. This
was only reasonable: Bradford's authority was deservedly
high, and Bradford had recorded the critical events from
which the New England myth was to be constructed. But
while *Of Plimmoth Plantation* deserved its eminence, the
loneliness of that eminence called attention to the flatness
of the surrounding landscape. New England historians
from Nathaniel Morton to Thomas Prince, from Cotton
Mather to Thomas Hutchinson, diligently consulted and
generously copied Bradford's manuscript: to check colonial historians of New England against one another is all
too often to check Bradford against Bradford. Piety for
Bradford was indeed reasonable, but it was also a symptom of resignation, a demonstration of the very decay that

would be the dominant theme of the histories written in the second half of the seventeenth century.

The very purpose of these histories was borrowed from the Founders. Bradford had made it plain that he was filling his history with circumstantial detail so that the Puritans' "children may see with what difficulties their fathers wrastled in going through these things in their first beginnings, and how God brought them along notwithstanding all their weaknesses and infirmities."[1] By the 1670's, the call for didactic history had become general, and its reasons were Bradford's reasons. But the tone had a new pathos. In 1672, the General Court of Massachusetts Bay Colony voted to encourage the collecting of special providences, of events "beyond what could in reason have binn expected," so that Puritans might be led to serve their Lord.[2] In the following year, Urian Oakes said in a famous plea: "It is our great duty to be the Lords *Remembrancers* or *Recorders*." God had been good to his children, and "it were very well if there were a memorial of these things faithfully drawn up, and transmitted to Posterity." Such a history of New England would register in men's hearts now, and remind later generations, how much the Lord had done for his elect. "It is a desirable thing, that all the loving kindnesses of God, and his singular favours to this poor and despised out cast might be Chronicled and communicated (in the History of

---

[1] Bradford, *Of Plymouth Plantation*, I, 120.

[2] Kenneth B. Murdock, "William Hubbard and the Providential Interpretation of History," *Proceedings of the American Antiquarian Society*, LII (1942), 23.

them) to succeeding Ages; that the memory of them may not dy and be extinct, with the present Generation."[3] And three years later, in 1676, Increase Mather pleaded the utility of history, the encouragement Scripture gives to its writing, and the propriety of divines to write it, as weighty support to his earnest wish that "some effectual Course may be taken (before it is too late) that a just *History of New England* be written and published to the World. That," he added, forgetful or disdainful of the histories already available, "is a thing that hath been often spoken of, but was never done to this day, and yet the longer it is deferred, the more difficulty will there be in effecting of it."[4]

Considering the frequency and solemnity of such calls for history, the response was tepid: if the American Puritans had any special vocation for history, they did not show it. Nathaniel Morton, Bradford's nephew and a diligent official in his own right, anticipated much of the public demand with his *New Englands Memoriall*, published in 1669, a compilation drawn largely from his uncle's manuscript. William Hubbard, the learned and urbane minister of Ipswich, discovered his historical talents with an effective history of the Indian wars, published in 1677, and then turned to a *General History of New England from the Discovery to MDCLXXX*; it closely followed Morton's *Memoriall* and Winthrop's

---

[3] *New-England Pleaded With* (1673), quoted in Miller and Johnson, *The Puritans*, I, 81.

[4] *A Brief History of the War with the Indians in New-England*, ed. Samuel G. Drake (1862), p. 37.

Journal, but took its own course with its relatively skeptical view of providential intervention in history. In 1682, the General Court voted to pay Hubbard £50 in support of this history, but it remained in manuscript: neither its intellectual dependence nor its theological independence, it seems, appeared an adequate answer to New England's need for a reliable past. The most alert, most obedient response to Increase Mather's invitation came from his son, Cotton Mather, who always responded to his father's invitations.

II

Cotton Mather's *Magnalia Christi Americana*, written between 1693 and 1697, and published in London in 1702, is an erudite, informative, sprawling, and puzzling book. It is extraordinarily ambitious: its subtitle, "The Ecclesiastical History of New England," though suggestive of its orientation, falls markedly short of its scope. In seven books, the *Magnalia* offers a cursory outline of New England's history from the Plymouth settlement to the end of the seventeenth century; a set of brief biographies of governors and other officials; a far larger set of far more massive biographies of "Famous Divines"—for, Mather said, "of all History it must be confessed, that the palm is to be given unto Church History; wherein the dignity, the suavity, and the utility of the subject is transcendent";[5] a history of "Harvard-Colledge" complete with the lives of some prominent ministers who graduated from

---

[5] Cotton Mather, *Magnalia Christi Americana*, I, 28.

it; the "Acts and Monuments" of the Puritan churches in America; a "Faithful Record" of "many Illustrious, Wonderful Providences" as they fell upon God's children in New England; and, in conclusion, a history of *"The Wars of the Lord,"* of Antinomians, Quakers, clerical impostors, and other plagues that beset the elect in the wilderness. Of all the Puritan intellectuals in New England in his time, only Cotton Mather could have written this history.

Cotton Mather has been widely, and often justly, maligned. If he had never existed, no village atheist would have had the wit to invent him. He was a seeker who drove the Puritan habit of self-examination, and the Puritan affliction of self-doubt, to morbid lengths: he writhed in the dust for his loathsome idleness after spending the day in exhausting charitable endeavor; weeping and praying, day after day, he looked for sure signs of grace; he performed in public as the omniscient guardian of morality while in private he moaned over his unclean soul; he tried to do justice to the leading role that his powerful father had assigned to him and, in a sense, acted out for him in his own versatile career, but, in the midst of success, surrounded by the trophies of his power, the son saw himself as a pathetic failure. Cotton Mather was singularly unfortunate in these symptoms: they display so much self-deception, so much self-indulgence, that they invite psychoanalytical probing, but without the clinical benevolence that the psychoanalyst extends to his patients. Cotton Mather lusted all his life for the presidency of Harvard, a post his father had held, and which the son affected to despise, especially after others were chosen; he was a prig and a meddler; an unscrupulous ideologue and a windy orator; a scribbler who praised simplicity in flowery circumlocutions, so anxious to see his productions in print that it might be said of him, with little fear of exaggeration, that he would rather lose his soul than misplace a manuscript.

Yet this same man, and without any apparent sense of strain, was also a patient husband and affectionate father; a responsible clergyman who gave generously of his time to counsel young people and new churches; an intelligent bibliophile and often discriminating reader; a curious observer of God's handiwork, interested enough in science to become a Fellow of the Royal Society—or, at least so eager for the right to bear the initials F. R. S. that he made extensive, if sometimes absurd, inquiries into nature. He was less responsible, and less courageous, in the witchcraft episode than some of his fellow Puritans, but also less credulous, and far less sadistic, than most of his fellow divines. He was, in sum, a cultivated man with a good mind and an international reputation. His stature, and his oddities, make him remarkable, but he was neither unique nor eccentric among the Puritans; what gives him significance is precisely that he was characteristic of his time and of his tribe.

It is Mather's representative quality that makes his *Magnalia* such an informative witness to the Puritan mind in America. Yet, though informative, it is also a reluctant witness: its meaning lies concealed in the maze of its organization and the tangled wilderness of its prose. Its opening line—"I write the WONDERS of the CHRISTIAN RELIGION, flying from the depravations of *Europe*, to the *American Strand*,"—evokes Vergil, but the rest of the book bears no resemblance to Vergil's classical balance and lovely melody. The *Magnalia* displays learning as Othello displayed love, not wisely but too well. No American writer has been called pedant more often than Cotton Mather, no American writer has deserved the epithet more than he. As early as 1708, the hostile English historian John Oldmixon recognized, and proclaimed, the literary limitations of the *Magnalia*: the book, he wrote, is "cramm'd with Punns, Anagrams, Acrosticks, Miracles and Prodigies."[6] Oldmixon was right: the *Magnalia* is a showcase of pedantry and elephantine wit. It is overloaded, and often overwhelmed, with expansive and irrelevant introductory passages, with far-fetched parallels, embarrassing puns, fatiguing alliterations, puerile anagrams; the writing is prolix, arch, involuted, imprecise, repetitive, and hysterical. It is also reactionary, a retreat to the ornate Mandarin writing fashionable half a century before. The *Magnalia*, as Oldmixon shrewdly observed, was like one of those "School Boys Exercises" of "Forty Years Ago."[7]

For all that, Mather prided himself on his style—another instance of his failure to achieve self-knowledge. He claimed that he had written his *Magnalia* in a "simple, submiss, humble style," and he never ceased to express his

---

[6] Quoted by Perry Miller, *The New England Mind: From Colony to Province* (1953), p. 360.
[7] *Ibid.*

affection for Puritan simplicity. In the *Magnalia* he promises to record the lives of Puritan divines without "figure of rhetorick";[8] he enjoys retelling the story of young John Cotton giving up metaphysical preaching and embracing the plain style after his conversion; and he holds up his grandfather Richard for his "way of preaching," which was "very plain, studiously avoiding obscure and foreign terms, and unnecessary citations of Latin sentences."[9] As the reader of the *Magnalia* knows, the grandson did not imitate his grandfather, at least not in this.

Yet there were times when Cotton Mather actually wrote well; in some of his scientific letters and didactic pamphlets, in several narrative passages in the *Magnalia* itself, he was direct, economical, even dramatic. But these felicitous passages only arouse the suspicion that Mather's style was more a symptom than a policy. His modes of writing appear not as the result of deliberate choices, but of irrational forces; Mather is not in control of his materials. His vacillations, his incoherence, like his profusion of words and deluge of allusions, suggest—it is no more than an impression—that Mather had something to hide, some besetting uncertainty, some fear of an unpalatable or unbearable truth, perhaps some doubt about the vocation of the Mather dynasty in God's New England.

The organization of the *Magnalia* strengthens this impression. Its seven books, as I have said, proceed from topic to topic, each in roughly chronological order.

---

8 *Magnalia Christi Americana*, I, 31.
9 *Ibid.*, I, 452.

Hence decisive events, like the expulsion of the Anti-nomians, the troubles at Harvard College, the execution of the Quakers, may be reported several times, or re-ported only in passing. Mather offers much documentary evidence—he reprints the Statutes of Harvard, and the resolutions of Synods, in full—and he does not shun nar-ration: he gives detailed descriptions of rescues at sea and battles with Indians. But over and over again Mather in-terprets critical moments in Puritan society as personal crises, social conflicts as the struggles of individual Chris-tians with Satan. Mather dissolves history into biography.

The result is strangely soothing, especially since the lives that Mather celebrates appear as almost wholly ad-mirable. Samuel Clark, the prolific English biographer whom Mather read with much interest though not with-out some reservations, had laid it down that the biog-rapher "must eye" his subjects "not to observe their weak-nesses, to discover their shame, for this is a poysonous dis-position"; but "eye them, as we look into Glasses, to dress, and adorn ourselves thereby." He "must eye them for imitation": he must "look upon the best, and the best in the best."[10] Cotton Mather cheerfully agreed. "How can the *lives* of the commendable be written without com-mending them?"[11] he asked, and answered his rhetorical question in 1,400 pages.

The scores of biographies that populate the *Magnalia*

[10] *Lives of Ten Eminent Divines* (1662), A3, quoted in Donald A. Stauffer, *English Biography Before 1700* (1930), p. 253.
[11] *Magnalia Christi Americana*, I, 30.

are indispensable to Mather's irenic strategy. They were a sound choice: in the seventeenth century, biographies enjoyed enormous popularity. They were the kind of history everyone could understand, and they permitted readers to measure themselves against giants or identify themselves with sufferers. Biography, wrote John Norton in his life of John Cotton, gave witness to "many full and glorious triumphs over the World, Sin and Satan, obtained by persons in like temptations, and subject to like passions with ourselves."[12] Such a genre simply could not fail. "When many excellent Lives are collected into one or more Volumes," Samuel Clark said confidently, "they do continue, and will do so, till Printing shall be no more."[13] Cotton Mather's *Magnalia Christi Americana* was a collection of excellent lives.

Cotton Mather was too great an admirer of his "incomparable Plutarch" to reduce his biographies to mere eulogies.[14] Mather knew everyone of consequence in New England, and he used his position intelligently: he secured private letters and intimate diaries, sought out eye-

---

[12] Kenneth B. Murdock, "Clio in the Wilderness: History and Biography in Puritan New England," *Church History*, XXIV (1955), 227. God himself, the American Puritans believed, had enjoined them to write history—had he not said, in the 140th Psalm, "He hath made his wonderful works to be remembered"? Murdock, *ibid.*, 222.

[13] See Stauffer, *English Biography Before 1700*, p. 305.

[14] Mather calls Plutarch "incomparable" in *Magnalia Christi Americana*, I, 29. In his life of Governor William Phips, Mather announces that he intends to imitate Plutarch's method as a biographer. *Ibid.*, I, 166.

witnesses, and then wove his precious materials into a coherent narrative. At the same time, Mather subordinated the individuality of his lives to their pedagogic purpose. He strove to entertain, but to entertain for the sake of giving instruction, and to instruct—as Samuel Clark, and before him, many other biographers, had said —for the sake of inducing imitation.

The biographies in the *Magnalia* are, therefore, exemplary lives, cut from a single pattern. A typical life runs somewhat like this: One: the young man converts to a religious walk of life, and his conversion is attended with deep misery and high illumination, lengthy turmoil and a tormenting conviction of unworthiness. Two: close study of Scriptures convinces him that Anglican ceremonies are affected with popish pomp, and Anglican beliefs laden with popish trash; the true Christian, he discovers, must be a Puritan, living, as all Puritans do, in the primitive simplicity of the early Church. Three: this conviction subjects him to harassment by hardened sinners, Satan's minions in England, and leads to his decision to flee to the American strand. Four: Laud's dreaded pursuivants try to capture the convert that they may torment him, but they are miraculously diverted from their prey. Five: the young Congregationalist crosses to America, and his passage is beset by dreadful storms and near disaster, but a special Providence—secured after fervent prayers—calms the sea and eases the voyage (at this point, the pattern provides an alternative: God grants his saint smooth passage to America). Six: once in New England, the saint performs wonderfully well in his calling, securing conversions, guarding the churches, keeping peace in the colony. Seven: when the time for settling down is ripe, the saint contracts a marriage that is a model of mutual devotion and Christian love, with husband cherishing wife and wife obeying husband—all marriages in New England, at least all marriages in the *Magnalia*, are blissfully happy. Eight: as he grows older, the saint leads an unspotted private life, bringing up grave—Mather's word is "old"—young men and women who are filled with concern for their salvation and the love of death, and showing worldly men the road to sobriety and devotion. Nine: since Satan never sleeps, the saint suffers repeated assaults of temptation, but fights them all off. Ten: the saint grows rich in years and honors, and dies an edifying death, commemorated by the poems of his friends, celebrated by the eulogy of his pastor, and witnessed by his tearful, unconsolable wife. Eleven: widow remarries.

This, Cotton Mather tells his readers over and over again, this is how men lived in New England, this is how they should live, but this is how they live no longer. Mather was the Plutarch of Puritan America, but he was a pathetic Plutarch. In an age of Jeremiads the *Magnalia Christi Americana* is the greatest Jeremiad of them all.

III

The second generation of American Puritans lived under the doom of divine displeasure. They were certain of it, largely because they incessantly confirmed each others' apprehensions. In 1662, "in the time of the great drought," Michael Wigglesworth found an appropriate designation for the Puritans' malaise; it was a sign, he said, of "God's Controversy with New-England."[15] To us, such a controversy appears as a projection, a sign of inner uncertainty. But to Wigglesworth, as to his fellow Puritans, it was an objective reality: Puritans had planted New England and prospered there, but now they were declining, living in the daily expectation of divine punishment. To be sure, New England still harbored "many praying saints"—to appeal to them was, after all, the point of Wigglesworth's poetic effort—but the saints must act before it was too late:

> Beware, O sinful land, beware;
> And do not think it strange
> That sorer judgments are at hand,
> Unless thou quickly change.

Wigglesworth was a pastor, but devout laymen echoed his judgment. "*New-England* is not to be found in *New-England*, nor *Boston* in *Boston*," Joshua Scottow, a prosperous businessman, wrote mournfully in 1691. "We must now cry out, our *Leanness*, our *Leanness*, our *Apostacy*, our *Atheism, Spiritual Idolatry, Adultery, Formality in Worship, carnal and vain Confidence* in Church-Privileges, forgetting of GOD our Rock, and Multitude of other

---

[15] A sizable selection from the poem is reprinted in Miller and Johnson, *The Puritans*, II, 611-616. My quotation below is at p. 616.

66

Abominations."[16] Everyone articulate enough to publish tracts or sermons agreed that spiritual decay was a pervasive rot, attacking New England at its roots, and inviting the most dreadful disasters; the cheerful remnant was silent. The General Court proclaimed official Days of Humiliation, and in its call compiled appalling lists of military defeats, bad harvests, epidemic outbreaks, interchurch rivalries, and untimely deaths. Puritan preachers above all, who had always found portentous warnings an entertaining theme for their sermons, specified for their parishioners the counts of the great indictment under which they all lay. Boston is the new Babylon, its fair face pockmarked with alehouses and whorehouses; merchants dream of profits and imperil their immortal souls; the rising generation forgets its obedience; shameless daughters of Zion parade about with naked arms and naked breasts; sinners drunk with prosperity imitate English fashions and invite the lightning by wearing periwigs. All these evils, and others, Increase Mather said in 1679, are "a sad sign that we have in great part forgotten our *Errand* in this Wilderness."[17]

The function of these laments was plain to performer and audience alike. The Jeremiad was a stylized history, designed to shame the present generation out of its erring ways by recalling the surpassing virtues of its fathers. The

---

[16] *Old Men's Tears for their own Declension mixed with Fears of their and Posterities Falling off from New England's Primitive Constitution*, quoted in Bernard Bailyn, *The New England Merchants in the Seventeenth Century* (1955), p. 123.

[17] Bailyn, *New England Merchants*, p. 141.

modern Jeremiah prayerfully expected that the celebration of the Founders would change the course of affairs
and prepare a future worth celebrating.

There was nothing new about this purposeful scolding;
in fact, it derived much of its strength from its respectable ancestry. The prophets of the Old Testament—and
not Jeremiah alone—had reminded their flocks of a heroic
time when men walked with God; urbane Greek poets
had composed their nostalgic pastorals to move their
readers to a purer life; Roman orators, historians and poets
had sought to cure the corruption and decadence of an
imperial city by constructing Republican fantasies about
courageous, simple men, and chaste, dutiful women. Like
their secular ancestors, the New England Jeremiahs as-
tutely mixed historical fact with edifying fiction; like
their religious ancestors, they impregnated their tirades
with mythical thinking. God, they insisted, was angry,
and manifested his anger with dire visitations. One way—
the Puritan divines thought the best, probably the only
way—of reconciling him to his children was to acknowl-
edge the visitations, to dwell on them with the kind of
pleasure that only self-punishment can give, to accept
them humbly, with real repentance, and to resolve to do
better. Doubtless there were some practicing Congregationalists who listened to these Jeremiads and enjoyed
them as a conventional ceremony; doubtless there were
others who used them unscrupulously to score debating
points against political opponents: it was all too easy to
see the hand of Satan in the maneuvering of a rival minister, and to interpret his prosperity as a visible token of

New England's decline. There were some, too, who took the Jeremiad as a rite of propitiation, hoping to avert the jealousy of higher powers by dramatizing the Puritans' afflictions, on the age-old principle that God humbles the happy. But most of the Jeremiads—and there were many —bear the unmistakable mark of absolute sincerity. They speak of decay because they see decay; they say that God's hand is on his sinful children because they see God's hand in Indians winning battles and beloved relatives dying young. The Jeremiad was a ritual and a remedy, but the ritual was grounded in the Puritans' most intimate convictions and most pressing anxieties, and the remedy was not prescribed lightly. For the devout Puritan in Cotton Mather's day, the enterprise of New England was sick unto death; the dismay of the aging John Winthrop and William Bradford had become the dominant temper of the orthodox.

The Jeremiads were implicit histories, the histories were explicit Jeremiads. Cotton Mather was perfectly clear about this. *"De tristibus,"* he said, "may be a proper title for the book I am now writing."[18] The book he wrote began with triumphant settlements, and with that magnificent invocation of Vergil; it ended with an account of afflictions, and a quotation from the most pathetic book of the Old Testament: "We have been under the lamentable punishments of our sins for two lustres of years together, 'tis time for every man, and for all of us as one man, to say, as in Lamentations iii, 40, 'Let us search

---

[18] *Magnalia Christi Americana*, II, 537.

and try our ways, and turn again unto the Lord.' "[19] To ask men to turn again unto the Lord suggests, plainly enough, that they have turned away from him. "I saw a fearful *degeneracy*," Mather intoned, adjusting the mantle of the Old Testament prophet around his shoulders, "creeping, I cannot say, but rushing in upon these churches; I saw to multiply continually our dangers, of our losing no small points in our *first faith*, as well as our *first love*, and of our giving up the *essentials* of that church order, which was the very end of these colonies; I saw a visible *shrink* in all orders of men among us, from that *greatness*, and that *goodness*, which was in the *first grain* that our God brought from *three sifted kingdoms*, into this land, when it was a *land not sown*."[20]

With the sure instinct of a trained polemicist, Mather couched his warnings in the commonplaces current among his peers: there was grave danger, he said, that New England might forget its *"errand into the wilderness"*;[21] it is "very certain," he said, that "the God of heaven had (and still hath!)" a "controversie" with New England.[22] In this emergency, Mather saw his duty. Obviously, *"speedy* care" must "be taken to preserve the memorables of our first settlement," lest the "laudable *principles* and *practices* of that first settlement" be utterly "lost in our apostasies." Mather resolves to recall, and by recalling revive primitive worship: "To advise you

---

[19] *Ibid.*, II, 681.
[20] *Ibid.*, I, 249.
[21] *Ibid.*, I, 64.
[22] *Ibid.*, II, 318.

of your dangers," he tells the churches of Connecticut, "and uphold the *life* of *religion* among you, I presume humbly to lay before you the life of that excellent man," Thomas Hooker. "What should be done for the stop, the turn of this degeneracy?" Mather asks himself, and replies: "I'll shew them the graves of their dead fathers."[23]

Obviously Mather's readers liked nothing better; the *Magnalia* soon acquired and long retained great authority. It was valuable enough to be stolen: in 1720, a burglar ransacking Jonathan Belcher's well-stocked warehouse included in his booty "a Book Entituled, Magnalia Christi Americana."[24] Approval such as this did not rest on shared necrophilia alone; the *Magnalia* told the Puritans what they wanted to hear. It told them, to begin with—and it was edifying to hear it from a philosopher who corresponded with savants in Europe—that the old theology, the theology of William Bradford and, indeed, St. Augustine, need not be revised in the light of modern knowledge. Moses still was, as he had always been, "the first and the best historian in the world."[25] God himself had cast "a long *series* of preserving and prosperous smiles" on the early settlers of New England, and now that "the enchantments of *this world*" had "caused the rising generation" to "neglect the primitive designs and interests of *religion* propounded by their fathers," God was blasting harvests, drowning sailors, burning houses, and filling the

---

[23] *Ibid.*, I, 249-252; I, 332.

[24] Clifford K. Shipton, *New England Life in the 18th Century*, p. 48, life of Jonathan Belcher.

[25] *Magnalia Christi Americana*, II, 109.

air with pestilence.[26] The marvelous stories about pious divines rescued at sea by a special Providence, the affecting stories about dying children converting their unregenerate fathers with the Lord's help, the fitting last words of convicted criminals led by God to say the appropriate thing, the poetic justice dealt out to blasphemers by a watchful and vengeful Lord—all these were true. The visible world, like the invisible world, was full of wonders.

This was reassuring enough. But the *Magnalia* did not stop here. It also told its readers that Puritan New England was important, its cause just, and its conduct irreproachable. Doubtless there were scoffers—there were always scoffers. "But whether *New-England* may Live any where else or no," Cotton Mather wrote, with slightly tremulous pride, "it must *live* in our *History*." Admittedly, "a war between *us* and a handful of Indians" may "appear no more than a *Batrachomyomachie* to the world *abroad*." But to New Englanders "*at home* it hath been considerable enough to make an history."[27] Thinking of his own *Magnalia*, Mather could feel confident that his modesty was misplaced: New England was considerable enough to make a history abroad as much as at home.

It deserved to live in history because it was fulfilling a great calling. Like other New England Jeremiahs, Cotton Mather had two masks: tragedy for domestic, comedy for foreign consumption. Of course, New England was de-

---

[26] *Ibid.*, II, 316.
[27] *Ibid.*, I, 27; II, 581.

caying: that was the point of the Jeremiads; of course, New England was imperfect: that was the nature of man. Still, New England remained a city upon a hill: "I perswade myself," Mather suavely observed, "that *so far as they have attained*," the Congregational churches in America "have given great examples of the methods and measures wherein an Evangelical Reformation is to be prosecuted." To be sure, "I do not say, that the Churches of New-England are the most *regular* that can be; yet I do say, and am sure, that they are very like unto those that were in the first ages of Christianity."[28] It was the highest praise Mather could bestow.

These complex judgments confirm the impression that Cotton Mather had something to hide. The *Magnalia* proves the Puritans guilty, and pronounces them innocent. Mather reaches this gratifying verdict by emphasizing consensus at the expense of conflict: he forgets inconvenient facts, refuses to call things by their right names, and defends the indefensible. It is possible to reconstruct the battles among the churches of New England by reading the *Magnalia* with infinite care, but infinite care is needed, for Mather calls this vicious internecine warfare, "little *controversies*."[29] In 1668, John Davenport, a founder of New Haven and pastor there, accepted a call from the First Church in Boston, despite his advanced age and despite the reluctance of his parishioners to let him go. His supporters in Boston suppressed

[28] *Ibid.*, I, 26-27.
[29] *Ibid.*, I, 63.

vital evidence to secure his appointment; Davenport himself, eager to sit in the place once graced by John Cotton, gave it as his opinion that "whither it be from errour in judgment" or from "designe," it was "evident Satan hath a great hand" in the resistance of his opponents.[30] The parishioners of the First Church, and with them the city of Boston, divided into vituperative factions; before it was all over, the minority had walked out and formed a congregation of their own—Old South Church. Of these proceedings, known to all, ugly in tone, unprecedented in acrimony, there is scarcely a trace in the *Magnalia*; Mather omits all specific details and instead says airily that Davenport's "removal from New Haven was clogged with many temptatious difficulties"—but then, would it not be a miracle if on so long a journey one did not meet some stumbling stones? And in any event, Davenport "broke through them all, in expectation to do what he judged would be a more comprehensive service unto the churches of *New-England*, than could have been done by him in his now undistinguished colony."[31] And so, an old man's ambition, and an undignified squabble, are transmuted into glorious service to God.

Vagueness is a favorite weapon of apologists, and Cotton Mather uses it with admirable deftness. He waves aside the fierce contentions among the Connecticut churches: "There arose at length some unhappy contests

---

[30] See Hamilton Andrews Hill, *History of the Old South Church (Third Church) Boston, 1669-1884*, 2 vols. (1890), I, 24.
[31] *Magnalia Christi Americana*, I, 328-329.

in one town of the colony, which grew into an alienation that could not be cured" without a bitter parting. Still, all was for the best: "These little, idle, angry *controversies*, proved occasions of *enlargements* to the church of God; for such of the inhabitants as chose a *cottage in a wilderness*," just moved "peaceably higher up the river, where a whole county of holy churches has been added unto the number of our congregations."[32] After this, it comes as no surprise to read Mather's bland biography of the subtle John Cotton, and Mather's expansive account of the Antinomian crisis, in which Cotton's prevarications are disguised behind a few portentous phrases and dissolved in a cheerful denouement: "An happy *conclusion of the whole matter*."[33] Retelling the career of William Bradford, obviously with the manuscript of *Plimmoth Plantation* before him, Mather has no difficulty seeing Reverend Lyford as a hypocrite, a liar, and a plotter—that, after all, is what Bradford had called him. But when it comes to Bradford's interception and opening of Lyford's letters to England—an illegal action which Bradford justifies in considerable detail—Mather improves on his source in the interest of making his saint more saintly: "At last there fell into the hands of the governour" Lyford's letters "home to England."[34]

---

[32] *Ibid.*, I, 83.

[33] *Ibid.*, II, 515. This incident had already been noted by Perry Miller in *The New England Mind: From Colony to Province*, p. 61.

[34] *Magnalia Christi Americana*, I, 60. Bradford's original account is in *Of Plymouth Plantation*, I, 382-388.

What Mather does not achieve with dilution, he achieves with suppression. Mather is uncomfortably aware that the treatment of the Quakers has given the American Puritans a bad name: "A great clamour hath been raised against New-England for their 'persecution of the Quakers.' " He refuses to defend it—"if any man will appear in the vindication of it, let him do as he please; for my part, I will not"—and then proceeds to defend it. He regrets the executions: "*Haereticide*" is not an "*evangelical way* for the extinguishing of heresies"; neglect, or contempt, would have been sufficient. Yet they were madmen, these Quakers, lunatics, energumens, enemies to the civil and sacred order of Massachusetts: the authorities, he is sure, would "gladly" have released them.[35] This is not unreasonable: the Quakers who came back to Massachusetts with full knowledge that their return would lead to their death were courting a martyr's fate. But Mather's account, though reasonable, is not candid: it is wholly silent about the poignant sufferings of the miserable sectaries, about the insults, the bloody whippings, the brutal legislation enacted expressly against them; it is largely silent about Governor John Endicott, that tight-lipped fanatic, who of all the Quakers' scourges in New England was the worst. Cotton Mather's impulse to decency was strong, but he could not afford to indulge it to the full. The Puritans wanted their myth, and Cotton Mather, obliging as always, supplied the demand.

---

[35] See especially, *Magnalia Christi Americana*, I, 298; II, 523-525.

IV

The *Magnalia Christi Americana* was tribal history, expressing Puritan sentiments, feeding Puritan anxieties, and sustaining Puritan pride. But it was also something more specific: it was family history constructed on the single principle that the Mathers were always right.

This principle is not as parochial as it may sound; in New England, as in old England, party history was family history writ large. The Mathers were a potent and far-flung dynasty—Cotton Mather never forgot that he was the grandson of Richard Mather and John Cotton— and while they were wrong to identify family wishes with the public good, they had every right to claim that their private interests were inextricably interwoven with public policy. There were no modern political parties in the New England of Cotton Mather's day; there were stable groupings and shifting coalitions, confused contests for power, for status and rewards, in which alliances were formed, dissolved, and reorganized. The alignments were as varied as the issues, and largely depended on them: they arose from struggles for grants of land, competition for profitable intimacy with English officials, quarrels within congregations, and, on occasion, abstract questions like toleration. Politics in Mather's day, as in our own, was a serious game in which suppressed passions found their outlet: ambitious men exercised their energies, and quarrelsome men gratified their lust for trouble, by competing for office. It was also a religious game: to say, as we must say, that Puritan politics was interest politics is not to say that it was secular politics. Most New Englanders, urbane Anglicans and plain Congregationalists alike, were deeply religious men, and could contest religious issues with as much fervor as economic ones—and more.

By the time Cotton Mather wrote his *Magnalia*, New England had transformed itself from a collection of rude settlements into a civilized, diversified community, complete with social and political conflict. New England was still underpopulated: by 1700, it had about 100,000 inhabitants—Boston, its commercial and intellectual capital, had about 7,000—and most of this population were simple farmers and craftsmen. Yet, hard as the orthodox Puritans tried to retain traditional simplicities, New England society was too large, too complex, too prosperous, too civilized, to resist the need for change. England, in those days of slow and hazardous travel, still seemed far away, but more and more as the century went on, it influenced affairs in its American dependencies. The great traumatic events in New England's history all occurred, or were all caused by events in England.

The early settlers had been singularly fortunate. They had built their Utopia with practically no interference from the home government—they had violated their charter, disregarded instructions from England, and in general conducted themselves like an independent power. But after the Restoration of Charles II, in 1660, this was no longer possible, and, to many New Englanders, no longer desirable. Merchants who developed extensive interests in international trade, gentry hungry for land and status, Anglican settlers who resented the Puritan monopoly of civic rights and political power, looked to England for protection, for profits, for comforts, for symbols of distinction. Merchants might be restive under the restrictions of the English Navigation Acts, but they preferred a remote monarchy that limited their profits to a watchful oligarchy that kept them politically impotent and socially insecure. The stirring events of the 1680's, culminating in a rather belated Glorious Revolution in New England in the Spring of 1689, realigned political alliances for a while: Puritan oligarchs, prosperous merchants, ambitious politicians found it expedient to make compromises, to cooperate under the new Protestant monarchy, and to work for the restoration of their Charter.

But while social groupings found uneasy peace in their demand for partial self-government and their search for a social organization capable of coping with new realities, the Puritan oligarchy itself was fatally divided. Protestantism has an irrepressible tendency toward fission; as Roman Catholics had argued since the sixteenth century, the exercise of private judgment must lead to the splintering of sects. The Puritan leadership in America had fully recognized this danger and had sought, at times desperately, to find the right middle way—some of the *Magnalia's* denials of trouble in paradise read like a frantic attempt to wish it out of existence. Yet, as the synods show by their Resolutions—by the very need to call them —the tensions inherent in Congregationalism could not be permanently kept down. Puritans prized religious experience but abhorred the chaos of private inspiration and unchecked enthusiasm; Puritans wished an orderly church but disliked the centralized authority of the Presbyterians. Puritans thought a church should be a gathering of saints, but they needed to insure its survival by admitting the saints' descendants: the uneasy and unenforceable compromise of the Half-Way Covenant, which they devised in the early 1660's—a procedure granting to children of church members who had had no saving religious experience of their own the right to all privileges of membership save only the Lord's Supper—was a symptom of their embarrassment. Puritans wanted no nonsense about toleration: why tolerate Satan? Yet there were many among them, and not among Cromwell's men alone, who hated persecution and thought many theological disagreements "indifferent," which is to say, harmless. Puritans accepted Calvin's uncompromising teachings about God's absolute sovereignty and man's total depravity, but their experience taught them that virtuous and vicious actions have their effect in the world and even on God: the Jeremiads were intended to have results, to change the mind of the Lord and the course of events.

Tentatively in the first generation, vigorously in the second, an increasing number of Puritans tried to resolve these tensions in what they liked to call a "Catholick spirit," a flexible attitude toward questions of doctrine, church polity, and the relations of the sacred to the secular power. They remained good Congregationalists; they believed in divine Providence, miracles, witches, and

Satan. But their temper was tolerant and expansive, and by the 1690's they were a distinct party, powerful enough to be recognized by Cotton Mather. "In my own country," he wrote in the *Magnalia*, there is "a number of eminently godly persons, who are for a larger way, and unto these my Church-History will give distaste."[36] It was not for this group that Mather wrote his history. "I have endeavoured, with all good conscience, to decline this writing meerly for a party,"[37] he proclaimed, but he was in fact writing for a party, and its head was named Mather.

This required some judicious navigation, for the Mathers had changed their minds. Increase Mather had first opposed, and then supported, the Half-Way Covenant; both Increase and Cotton Mather had accepted toleration with reluctance: it was imposed on them partly by developments in the New England churches, largely by the Glorious Revolution. In the *Magnalia*, Cotton Mather reports the first reversal as a blessing, and antedates the second reversal to give the Mathers credit they did not deserve.[38] The *Magnalia* was more than an apology for the Mather clan—it derived its persuasiveness from the excellence of much of its research and documentation. But in the end, the apologetic aim of the *Magnalia* overwhelms its historical scholarship, and it becomes a Jeremiad in the service of a tribe in retreat.

---

[36] *Ibid.*, I, 36.

[37] *Ibid.*, I, 29.

[38] See Perry Miller, *The New England Mind: From Colony to Province*, pp. 103, 108.

V

This interpretation of Cotton Mather and his most famous book may seem uncharitable. Did not the *Magnalia* itself show traces of a Catholick temper? Was it not, besides, a young man's work? Did not Mather's conduct, in the thirty years that remained to him, reveal a flexible spirit? Was it not a manifestation of admirable tolerance to have Mather preach at the ordination of a Baptist minister? Did he not show a progressive mentality during the inoculation controversy of 1721-1722, when he bravely stood by science and reason? Did he not write *The Christian Philosopher*, a pioneering work in natural theology which (in Kenneth Murdock's words) expounded an "advanced intellectual position" that looked forward to Emerson, offered "proof positive of his intellectual development," and proved "him to have been far more 'modern' than his times"?[39]

The facts are true enough, but they will not bear the strain that our historical piety places on them. To be sure—I have insisted on it—Cotton Mather was civilized, intelligent, and often reasonable. He had nothing but distaste for the more egregious forms of fanaticism; especially in his mature years, his pronouncements on religious toleration were irenic for temperamental, not merely for political reasons. He abhorred heresy, but he preferred combating it by persuasion to stamping it out

---

[39] Kenneth B. Murdock, ed., *Cotton Mather, Selections* (1926), pp. l-lii.

by force. His cultivation, the fruit of wide reading and high ambition, compelled him into a certain breadth of view. But none of these qualities made him a modern man. Not even his celebrated appearance in a Baptist church in 1718 justifies our calling him more modern than his times: he went to perform his good deed mainly to gratify his vanity; he was eager to bear "a Testimony to the grand Intention of an Union for good Men upon the Maxims of Piety" by ordaining a Baptist pastor, but he luxuriated in the awareness that his action would "cause much Discourse and Wonder," and "occasion various Discourse in the world."[40]

There was nothing that caused more discourse in the world of Boston than Cotton Mather's defense of inoculation. When the smallpox visited New England in 1721, Boylston inoculated a number of Bostonians, and Cotton Mather, to the dismay of many, supported him. Someone threw a bomb into Mather's house, and this bomb— which did not go off—has made him into a martyr to progress.[41] But the issue was not between science and superstition: most of the leading physicians, and many educated Puritans, thought inoculation an absurd and dangerous fad: Dr. William Douglass, who led the medical opposition, likened Mather's support of inoculation to Mather's support of the witchcraft trials thirty years before—another instance of "mistaken Notions." Mather was on the right side, and for good reasons: he had

---

[40] Cotton Mather, *Diary*, II, 531-536.
[41] See *ibid.*, II, 657-658.

first read of inoculation in the *Philosophical Transactions*. But he supported the practice in the spirit of a Christian virtuoso, certain that to cure a great evil by enduring a lesser one was to obey the ways of Providence: Increase Mather had discovered, and Cotton Mather rejoiced to see, that among those who approved of inoculation, only a few were men of "a Prophane Life and Conversation," while on the contrary, "it cannot be denied, but that the known Children of the Wicked one, are generally fierce Enemies to Inoculation."[42] To support inoculation under these circumstances was not to advance secularism but to combat Satan.

Cotton Mather wrote his *Christian Philosopher* in the same combative mood. If the book was indeed the first defense of natural theology in Puritan America, this reflects not the modernity of Mather but the provinciality of the Puritans. To prove the existence, the goodness, the glory, and the omnipotence of God by pointing to his manifestations in nature, to suggest that God had revealed himself first by his works and then by his words, was to utter an antique commonplace of Christian apologetics—and a safe one: Mather was at one with other apologists in insisting that natural religion taught not naturalism but humble submission to God's splendid decrees: "A PHILOSOPHICAL RELIGION: And yet how *Evangelical!*"[43]

---

[42] John B. Blake, "The Inoculation Controversy in Boston: 1721-1722," *New England Quarterly*, XXV (1952), 497, 503.

[43] *The Christian Philosopher*, Introduction, in Murdock, *Cotton Mather, Selections*, p. 286.

Such philosophical religion had deep roots in the books that the Puritans studied with unwearied devotion. "The heavens declare the glory of God; and the firmament sheweth his handy-work. Day unto day uttereth speech, and night unto night sheweth knowledge."[44] Thus the Psalmist. "For the invisible things of him from the creation of the world are clearly seen, being understood by the things that are made, even his eternal power and Godhead; so that they"—the ungodly and the unrighteous—"are without excuse."[45] Thus St. Paul to the Romans. The great Reformers, for all their insistence on divine sovereignty and inscrutability, all their preachment of the arbitrariness of Providence, commented on these Biblical passages with pious approval. Calvin above all insisted that "the knowledge of God shines forth in the fashioning of the universe and the continuing government of it," so that everyone must see his splendor: "The clarity of God's self-disclosure strips us of every excuse" for denying his "wonderful wisdom." It is not only astronomy, medicine, and other sciences intended to elucidate "recondite matters" that declare God's handiwork, but common, ordinary experiences, "which thrust themselves upon the sight of even the most untutored and ignorant person."[46] In 1728, in their obituary sermons, polite

---

[44] Psalm 19:1; see also Psalms 104 and 145.

[45] Romans 1:20.

[46] Calvin, *Institutes of the Christian Religion*, transl. by Ford Lewis Battles, ed. John T. McNeill, 2 vols. (1960), I, 51-53. In his exposition, Calvin relies mainly on Romans 1:20, Psalm 104, and Psalm 145.

Catholick preachers like Benjamin Colman found much to praise in Cotton Mather; but after all, there was much to praise, and besides, he was safely dead.[47] Yet the politeness of the eulogies could not conceal the distance of the new Congregationalists from the Mather faction. Far from looking ahead to Emerson's transcendentalism, Mather's thought looked back to the Church Fathers.

Cotton Mather had known this. He had found it expedient to reach an accommodation with the Colmans and the Brattles, but in December 1699, when the Brattle Street Church was being founded, the irreconcilable conflict found expression in Mather's diary. The Brattle Street group, he wrote, are "Head-strong Men," filled with "malignity to the Holy Wayes of our Churches"; these "fallacious people" delude "many better-meaning Men," and "invite an ill Party thro' all the Countrey, to throw all into Confusion." It was necessary to take strong action against these innovators, though even the most loving reproof only "enrages their violent and impotent Lusts, to carry on the *Apostasy*." These were strong words, but more was to come. In January of 1700, Cotton Mather confided to his diary that he saw "*Satan* beginning a terrible Shake unto the Churches of *New England*"; a "*Day of Temptation*" has come, brought by men who are "ignorant, arrogant, obstinate, and full of

---

[47] In his laudatory essay on Cotton Mather (Introduction to *Cotton Mather, Selections*), Kenneth Murdock quotes the opinions of Benjamin Colman, Thomas Prince, and Joshua Gee, all favorable, but all uttered upon Cotton Mather's death. It is well to remember Samuel Johnson's observation that "In lapidary inscriptions a man is not upon oath."

Malice and Slander," men who "fill the Land with *Lyes*."[48]

These are the rages of a defeated man, and indeed, Cotton Mather lost battle after battle. The merchants who put profits before piety, built lavish establishments, and married their daughters to Anglicans, founded the commercial empires that moved the colonies into active competition with European traders. The politicians who discounted religious considerations in their struggle for office or their zeal for good administration broke the tribal mould of Puritan society. The Catholick Congregationalists who founded Brattle Street Church, seized Harvard College from the Mathers, and moved, however timidly, toward Arminianism, opened the windows of a provincial society to the breezes of intellectual change, and prepared educated Americans for a fruitful reunion with enlightened Europe.

Yet Cotton Mather and, through him, Puritan orthodoxy, had their revenge. For two centuries and even longer, Americans, even those who criticized the *Magnalia* or professed to despise its author, have seen the great struggle for New England's soul through Cotton Mather's eyes. Everyone owned his history, everyone read it, everyone, consciously or not, absorbed its views and employed its categories. For whatever the liberals and rebels in Massachusetts did—and they did much— there was one thing they neglected to do. They did not write history.

---

[48] Cotton Mather, *Diary*, I, 325-326, 330.

Chapter Four

Jonathan Edwards

An American Tragedy

I

IN 1739, Jonathan Edwards delivered a series of sermons on the work of redemption, a breathtaking survey of the "grand design of God" in the "form of a history."[1] It was an audacious undertaking, unprecedented in the rich theological literature produced by the Puritans in America. Beset on one side by the enthusiasm of the Great Awakening and on the other by the threat of formal religiosity and frigid rationalism, Edwards rose to an Olympian view of man's religious destiny, and spoke to his flock at Northampton about things of the last importance: Christ's activity in behalf of man from the invention of time to its abolition. He was invading

---

[1] Jonathan Edwards to the Trustees of the College of New Jersey, October 19, 1757. *The Works of President Edwards*, 4 vols. (1847 and several times thereafter), I, 48.

treacherous territory, last traversed half a century before by the great Bossuet.[2]

Edwards, like Bossuet, was a professional theologian and only an amateur historian. But, like Bossuet, Edwards saw no reason to apologize for his excursion; he was only doing his duty. After all, "The work of REDEMPTION is a work that GOD carries on from the fall of man to the end of the world";[3] it was work God performed in, and through history, and what was more urgent for man than to trace evidences of that divine work in time? Besides, and from this motive, devout historical study had long been one of Edwards' favorite pursuits. "My heart has been much on the advancement of Christ's kingdom in the world," he observed in his spiritual autobiography. "When I have read histories of past ages, the pleasantest thing in all my reading has been, to read of the kingdom of Christ being promoted." The very anticipation of coming upon such a passage was a source of rejoicing. "My mind," he said, "has been much entertained and delighted with the Scripture promises and prophecies, which relate to the future glorious advancement of Christ's kingdom upon earth."[4]

---

[2] Thomas Prince, it is true, published his *Chronological History of New England, In the Form of Annals*, in 1736, and it begins with Adam, "year one, first month, sixth day." But he ends with 1630, and eschatological speculation is wholly absent from it.

[3] *A History of the Work of Redemption* (first published in 1774), in *Works*, I, 298.

[4] *Personal Narrative*, probably written in 1740, a year after the sermons on the work of redemption. *Works*, I, 21.

This pious, purposeful pleasure in history never left him. He importuned his European correspondents to send him the latest books on history and theology, and he continued to brood on his sermons on redemption: as late as October 1757, eighteen years after these sermons, he told the trustees of New Jersey College that he was not sure he wanted to be president of their institution, partly because his health was uncertain, partly because his learning was sadly incomplete, but largely because he was thinking of writing a *History of the Work of Redemption*. This history had been on his "mind and heart" for many years; he had begun it "long ago, not with any view to publication." It was to be a "great work," designed on "an entire new method"—towering claims for a man who, though he knew his powers, was a modest man—a work that would consider "the affair of Christian Theology, as the whole of it, in each part, stands in reference to the great work of redemption by Jesus Christ." Since the work of redemption, Edwards wrote, was the "*summum* and *ultimum* of all the divine operations and decrees; particularly considering all parts of the grand scheme, in their historical order," his book on redemption must be on a grand scale: it must look at "all three worlds, heaven, earth, and hell," and introduce "all parts of divinity in that order which is most scriptural and most natural."[5]

This program delighted Edwards: he was never afraid

---

[5] Edwards to the Trustees of the College of New Jersey, *ibid.*, I, 48-49.

of grand architectonic designs. His plan appeared to him "the most beautiful and entertaining, wherein every divine doctrine will appear to the greatest advantage, in the brightest light, in the most striking manner, shewing the admirable contexture and harmony of the whole."[6] In the enforced solitude of his later years, Edwards wrote some ambitious books and spun out some ambitious plans, but among all his works, realized or contemplated, his history of the work of redemption was the most ambitious. He did not live to write it; in March, 1758, he died, shortly after receiving inoculation for smallpox, a victim of modern science.

We can only speculate how Edwards would have transformed his sermons on redemption into a book of history. This much is certain: he would not have discarded, or modified, their classical Puritan theology. The books, the journals, and letters of his late years, like those of his early years, betray no skepticism of miracles, no doubt of Scripture, no rebellion against God's sovereignty, no deviation from the Augustinian vision of history. In the midst of the greatest revolution in the European mind since Christianity had overwhelmed paganism, Edwards serenely reaffirmed the faith of his fathers.

He had some notion that such a revolution was going on: he even read David Hume and professed himself "glad of an opportunity to read such corrupt books, especially when written by men of considerable genius"; it gave

---

[6] *Ibid.*, I, 49.

him, he said, "an idea of the notions that prevail in our nation."[7] But he had no idea how extensive that revolution was, and how far his own historical thinking deviated from the historical thinking about to seize control of educated opinion in Europe. In fact, the nineteen years between Edwards' sermons and Edwards' death were decisive years in the rebellion of the Enlightenment against Christianity. Hume published the first two books of his *Treatise of Human Nature* in 1739; Condillac his *Essai sur l'origine des connaissances humaines* in 1746; Montesquieu his *Esprit des lois* in 1748, and with these books the foundations for the Enlightenment's epistemology, psychology, and sociology were firmly laid down. They were all attempts (in David Hume's words) "to introduce the experimental Method of Reasoning into Moral Subjects";[8] attempts to found the science of man on the ideas of Locke and the method of Newton. They were scientific rather than metaphysical, critical rather than credulous, naturalistic in temper, and wholly incompatible with revealed religion of any kind.

History, ready as always to follow the new currents, was beneficiary, and part, of the offensive of the secular against the Christian mind. In the late 1730's, while Edwards was displaying to his congregation the activity of Christ in history, Voltaire was at work on his *Siècle de Louis XIV*, a book which, with its anticlericalism, its

---

[7] See Thomas H. Johnson, "Jonathan Edwards' Background of Reading," *Publications of the Colonial Society of Massachusetts*, XXVIII (1931), 210-211.

[8] Subtitle of Hume's *Treatise of Human Nature* (1739-1740).

worldliness, and its aggressive modernity, became the manifesto, and the model, of the new history. A few years later, Voltaire began his vast *Essai sur les mœurs*, the Enlightenment's answer to Bossuet. Both of these books were published in Edwards' lifetime: the first in 1751, the second in 1756. Hume turned to historical subjects in the late 1740's; he started work on his *History of England* in 1752, and four years later published its first installment, covering the Stuart dynasty from the accession of James I to the expulsion of James II. William Robertson, the great Scottish historian whose reputation then was higher than it is now, began the first of his masterpieces, the *History of Scotland*, in 1753. Edward Gibbon, who combined the secular mentality of the *philosophes* with the technical competence of the *érudits*, was still a young man in those years, but he had already found his vocation, perfected his classical learning, and discovered his religious position; all he needed was a subject commensurate with his talents, and he found that, with the lucid finality of a religious conversion, in 1764, only five years after Edwards' death.

To turn from these books to Edwards' *History of the Work of Redemption* is to leave the familiar terrain of the modern world with its recognizable features and legible signposts for a fantastic landscape, alive with mysterious echoes from a distant past, and intelligible only—if it can be made intelligible at all—with the aid of outmoded, almost primitive maps. The *philosophes'* histories made secular propaganda by providing information about a real past; Edwards' history made religious propaganda by arousing memories of a religious myth. To grasp the temper of Voltaire's or Hume's histories, one must read the new philosophy and collections of state papers; to grasp the temper of Edwards' history, one must read the Church Fathers and the Scriptures. However magnificent in conception, however bold in execution, Edwards' *History of the Work of Redemption* is a thoroughly traditional book, and the tradition is the tradition of Augustine.

The very plan of the book places it in this tradition. Edwards periodizes world history by relying wholly on sacred numbers and sacred events. The first great period stretches from the Fall of Man to the Incarnation of Christ; the second, from His Incarnation to His Resurrection; the third, from His Resurrection to the end of the world. The first of these great periods, in turn, is subdivided into six "lesser periods": from the Fall to the flood, the flood to the calling of Abraham, Abraham to Moses, Moses to David, David to the Babylonian Captivity, and the Captivity to the Incarnation.[9] The second period, Christ's short sojourn on this earth, need not be subdivided: it is an intense, luminous, concentrated moment in the career of God's world: "Though it was but between thirty and forty years, yet more was done in it than had been done from the beginning of the world to that time."[10] The third and last period, finally, matches

---

[9] *History of the Work of Redemption, Works,* I, 306.

[10] *Ibid.,* I, 395. Edwards does subdivide this period, but only for purposes of analysis.

the first in perfect symmetry; it is marked by six steps in "Christ's coming in his kingdom": from the Resurrection to the destruction of Jerusalem; the destruction of Jerusalem to the advent of the Christian Emperor Constantine; Constantine to the reign of Roman Catholicism; the reign of Antichrist to the Reformation; the Reformation to the present; the present to the final overthrow of Antichrist.[11]

This periodic scheme is the appropriate, indeed the only possible scheme for Edwards: it mirrors, and perfectly expresses, his theory of historical causation and historical purpose, and his prediction of the end of time. Edwards insists that the course of events follows a predetermined plan laid down by God before the Fall, indeed before Creation. God settled everything at the beginning: man's nature, man's sin, Satan's interference, Christ's intercession; and God settled it for the sole purpose of glorifying himself. In good Calvinist fashion, Edwards despised the doctrine of foreknowledge as the refuge of timid Christians: of course, God had perfect foreknowledge of man's future conduct, but if he had dictated the course of history merely because he knew what was going to happen, he could not be said to have dictated it, but merely to have conformed his decree to necessity. This was a limitation on the divine omnipotence to which Jonathan Edwards could never assent: no theme is more

---

[11] This periodization of the third period is less obvious than the first; it is, however, implicit. See C. C. Goen, "Jonathan Edwards: A New Departure in Eschatology," *Church History*, XXVIII (1959), 26.

consistent in his writings than the lovely and unlimited glory of God, which looks to the perfection of the creature for the sake of the perfection of the Creator: because God "infinitely values his own glory, consisting in the knowledge of himself, love to himself, and complacence and joy in himself; he therefore valued the image, communication or participation of these, in the creature. And it is because he values himself, that he delights in the knowledge, and love, and joy of the creature; as being himself the object of this knowledge, love and complacence."[12]

The historical drama, therefore, was divine in all its aspects; "this lower world," in which human history took place, "was doubtless created to be a stage."[13] God was author of the drama, its director, chief actor, and, just to make sure, authoritative critic. Everything had happened precisely as Scripture described it, everything would happen precisely as Scripture prophesied it: the past fulfillment of prophecies was guarantee, if guarantees were needed, of future fulfillment of prophecies not yet realized. The course of history did more than merely offer evidence in support of the divine origins of the Bible: the Bible was incomparably the most accurate and most sublime—in fact the only accurate and sublime—history ever written.

For Edwards, secular history was on the whole insig-

---

[12] *Dissertation Concerning the End For Which God Created the World, Works*, II, 256.

[13] *History of the Work of Redemption, Works*, I, 300.

nificant, or significant only as it illustrated, illuminated, impinged upon sacred history: kings appear only as they establish, or obstruct, the true church, wars are mentioned only as they serve to spread, or to constrict, the true faith. All of parts one and two, and much of part three, of the *History of the Work of Redemption* consists of a free retelling of Scripture, with each miraculous event reported as a historical event. For Edwards, the authority of the Bible is absolute. "There were many great changes and revolutions in the world, and they were all only the turning of the wheels of Providence in order to this, to make way for the coming of Christ, and what he was to do in the world. They all pointed hither, and all issued here."[14] Characters in the Old Testament acted in behalf of purposes greater than themselves, and prefigured great events of which they knew nothing, but they were real people, real historical subjects. There was an Adam and an Eve, and they sinned and awoke to their sense of guilt; there was a Cain and an Abel, a Noah and a Moses, and while they were symbols and types, they were symbols and types in the way all creaturely beings represent both themselves and God's intentions. In the modern sense, in the sense of Voltaire and Hume, almost none of Edwards' history is history—it is Calvinist doctrine exemplified in a distinct succession of transcendent moments.

Yet history intrudes. In the time span between the establishment of the primitive church and the apocalyptic future, the Bible provides no guidance; Edwards thus had

---

[14] *Ibid.*, I, 305.

to find other guides for the period between the first and the eighteenth centuries, and he found them in expected places. The style is the style of Jonathan Edwards, the story is the story told by Cotton Mather, by William Bradford, by John Foxe: in its first three centuries on earth, the true church was pure but suffered under persecution; then came years of prosperity and peace, as Constantine delivered the church from its travail—Satan, "the prince of darkness, that king and god of the Heathen world," was driven out.[15] But this time of rest did not last long: "Presently after, the church again suffered persecution from the Arians; and after that, Antichrist rose, and the church was driven away into the wilderness, and was kept down in obscurity, and contempt, and suffering for a long time."[16] While the true church was kept down, Satan's counterfeit church ruled the world: "The Pope and his clergy robbed the people of their ecclesiastical and civil liberties and privileges," and, just as Scripture had foretold, "robbed them of their estates, and drained all Christendom of their money, and engrossed the most of their riches into their own coffers, by their vast revenues, besides pay for pardons and indulgences, baptisms, and extreme unctions, deliverance out of purgatory, and a hundred other things." This renewed reign of Satan made "superstition and ignorance" prevail more than ever, for the Pope and his minions "industriously promoted ignorance"; in a line that David Hume

---

15 *Ibid.*, I, 450.
16 *Ibid.*, I, 438.

might have written—and in fact did write, almost word for word—Edwards reminded his congregation that it was "a received maxim" among the Papists that "ignorance is the mother of devotion: and so great was the darkness of those times, that learning was almost extinct in the world."[17] Finally, after many centuries, Satan was driven away once again, by the "reformation of Luther and others."[18] Here was a splendid moment in the history of God's own church: "God began gloriously to revive his church again, and advance the kingdom of his Son, after such a dismal night of darkness as had been before." There had been many endeavors by the witnesses to the truth, "for a reformation before," but it was only now, "when God's appointed time was come"—for in God's drama, all actors spoke their lines only on cue—that God's "work was begun, and went on with a swift and wonderful progress."[19]

Still, Edwards warned his flock, deliverance was not yet, and complacency was misplaced. The spirit of a true Christian remained what it had always been, a "spirit of suffering."[20] Satan, though wounded, was far from dead. He had risen higher and higher, and now felt himself falling once again, halfway to ruin, and with his last

---

[17] *Ibid.*, I, 458. Hume quotes the maxim, *"Ignorance is the mother of Devotion"* in his *The Natural History of Religion*, in *Philosophical Works*, 4 vols., eds. T. H. Green and T. H. Grose (1882), IV, 363.

[18] *History of the Work of Redemption, Works*, I, 438.

[19] *Ibid.*, I, 462.

[20] *Ibid.*, I, 479.

strength did his all to obstruct the great work of reformation. He strengthened the Papists through a great council, he fostered plots and conspiracies, he oppressed helpless minorities of true believers, he warred upon God's children. "The Heathen persecution had been very dreadful; but now persecution by the church of Rome was improved and studied, and cultivated as an art or science."[21] There was a time—a time that very old members of Edwards' congregation would remember—when Rome seemed near a decisive triumph: the king of England and "Lewis XIV. of France," both of them fanatical Papists, mounted a great conspiracy to extirpate what they called "the Northern heresy." But then, "just as their matters seemed to be come to a head, and their enterprise ripe for execution, God, in his providence, suddenly dashed all their schemes in pieces by the Revolution, at the coming in of King William and Queen Mary; by which all their designs were at an end; and the Protestant interest was more strongly established, by the crown of England's being established in the Protestant house of Hanover, and a Papist being, by the constitution of the nation, forever rendered incapable of wearing the crown of England. Thus they groped in darkness at noon-day as in the night, and their hands could not perform their enterprise, and their kingdom was full of darkness, and they gnawed their tongues in pain."[22] Like Cotton Mather before him, Jonathan Edwards distrusted the Anglican church, but he

---

21 *Ibid.*, I, 465.
22 *Ibid.*, I, 464.

accepted as divinely ordained the aid of an Anglican state against the Papists.

Such victories, though impressive, were not final. A candid survey of the modern world showed Satan at work in many places. Protestants had been expelled from Bohemia and from France not long before; "Ireland has been as it were overwhelmed with Protestant blood," and there had been cruel persecutions elsewhere.[23] "Thus did the devil and his great minister Antichrist, rage with such violence and cruelty against the church of Christ! And thus did the whore of Babylon make herself drunk with the blood of the saints and martyrs of Jesus!"[24] But Satan was serpent as well as Moloch, a subtle deceiver as well as a ravening monster, and the progress of the true church had been much impeded by the spreading of corrupt opinions: Arminianism has "greatly prevailed" in the Church of England and among dissenters, and "spread greatly in New England, as well as Old."[25] Deism, which denied revelation altogether, had "very much overrun" the English nation on both sides of the Atlantic—"our nation."[26] Perhaps worst of all, indifference to religion was spreading. "The glorious outpouring of the Spirit of God that accompanied the first Reformation" had greatly diminished, and "vital piety" was now despised as "*enthusiasm, whimsy,* and *fanaticism.*" Those who are truly religious, "are commonly looked upon to be crack-brained, and

---

23 *Ibid.*, I, 466.
24 *Ibid.*
25 *Ibid.*, I, 467.
26 *Ibid.*

beside their right mind; and vice and profaneness dreadfully prevail, like a flood which threatens to bear down all before it."[27]

But, as Edwards knew, it was not written that the threat should become reality. The future, being the future, was hard to fathom, the history of the future hard to write. But Edwards ventured to undertake it; armed with the book of Revelation and with his interpretation of some events in his own day, he projected his history forward to give hope to the saints in his audience, and to inspire the sinners with despair. There will be a time of darkness, then the millennium will come, then a final paroxysm of Satanic fury, and then the Judgment, the end of time, the end of history. "These sayings are faithful and true," Edwards said in conclusion, appropriately ending his cycle of sermons by paraphrasing the last chapter of Revelation, "and blessed is he that keepeth these sayings. Behold, Christ cometh quickly, and his reward is with him, to render to every man according as his work shall be. And he that is unjust, shall be unjust still; and he that is filthy, shall be filthy still; and he that is holy, shall be holy still. Blessed are they that do his commandments, that they may have right to the tree of life, and may enter in through the gates into the city: for without, are dogs, and sorcerers, and whoremongers, and murderers, and idolaters, and whatsoever loveth and maketh a lie. He that testifieth these things, saith, Surely I

---

[27] *Ibid.*, I, 471.

come quickly. Amen; even so come, Lord Jesus."[28]

Yes, Jesus would surely come. But when? Here, Edwards could remind his congregation of what they knew: there was an expectancy in the air, a self-satisfied prosperity among men of learning puffed with pride and self-sufficiency, an atmosphere reminiscent of the time around the first coming of Christ, when the pride of scholars was humbled by the divine foolishness. Besides, persecutions had lately much diminished, the wings of the Pope had been clipped, in Germany the blessed work of *"August Herman Frank"* testified that true piety was still alive. And then there was America, that vast continent so long wholly delivered over to the devil, yet recently gloriously receptive to the word of Christ: "Something remarkable has appeared of late here, and in other parts of America, among many Indians, of an inclination to be instructed in the Christian religion." Even Northampton could testify to the progress of Christ in this day: "Another thing, which it would be ungrateful in us not to take notice of, is that remarkable pouring out of the Spirit of God which has been of late in this part of New England, of which we, in this town, have had such a share." This was not egotism, not parochialism, not patriotism: Edwards only meant to suggest that small events were microcosms of great events, that an insignificant town might become the scene for a decisive transformation, that an obscure pastor might be the spokesman for a historic turning point. *The*

---

[28] *Ibid.*, I, 516.

History of the Work of Redemption makes no special claims for New England, for Northampton, or for Edwards; it claims only for all of these their rightful share in the divine drama.[29]

If Edwards had been an ordinary Congregationalist pastor, his history would be remarkable only for its range and its style: its underlying philosophy offers no surprises. But Edwards was a brilliant scholar, a gifted student of science, a deft dialectician; he read as widely as Cotton Mather and to greater profit; he was open to the most abstruse and most advanced works of philosophy; he was among the first in the New England colonies to study Locke and appreciate Newton. His mind was the opposite of reactionary or fundamentalist. Yet his history was both. Such apparent contradictions are a sign of something extraordinary; with Jonathan Edwards, they are the mark of tragedy.

II

When we speak of Jonathan Edwards, we are bound to speak of tragedy—perhaps all too easily. Certainly his philosophy was not tragic: it was Calvinist. Edwards was aware of man's limits and limitations, of man's futile striving, his anguish and his defeats, and these are prominent themes in authentic tragedy. But they are not of its es-

---

[29] See *ibid.*, I, 468-470. This (as one of my listeners correctly pointed out) does not mean that Edwards was wholly immune to local pride—he was not. But his conviction that he, and New England, had a special place in the providential scheme was at best—or at worst—expressed only on rare occasions.

sence. The tragic situation arises when a man of stature produces, through his actions, great conflict and great suffering. The conflict may be between the imperious urge of passion and the lucid restraint of reason, between two high but irreconcilable duties, between a corrupt society and an honorable innocent individual. However flawed he may be, the tragic hero must be neither villainous nor mediocre, and if he fails, as he is likely to, he must fail nobly, affirming the essential dignity, the essential autonomy, of his human estate. Even if God, or a god, enters the tragic action, the human hero remains the hero. But Edwards set man's historical situation into a supernatural frame: man is helpless in the hands of God, incapable of resisting the influx of grace or the decree of condemnation. The Calvinist drama—it is worth saying once again—is wholly predestined: its resolution—eternal salvation or eternal damnation—is unaffected by the actions of men, and takes place not in this world but in the next. That is why Calvinism, like other Christian philosophies, but far more than they, is alien to tragedy.

But while Calvinism is not a tragic system, Calvinists may become tragic heroes, and Jonathan Edwards was the greatest tragic hero—I suspect, the only tragic hero—that American Calvinism produced. Edwards' stature was commanding, his fate inevitable; his failure evokes both pity and admiration. His heritage and his spiritual travail had nothing unusual about them: other sons of Congregationalist pastors followed their fathers into the ministry, other Congregationalist pastors endured an invincible sense of their vileness interspersed with moments of euphoric participation in Christ. But with Jonathan Edwards, such commonplace experiences rose to a high pitch of intensity: he was more intelligent—much more intelligent—than the others, suffered more poignantly—or at least more articulately—than they, probed the meaning of Puritanism more persistently than anyone. As a young man, he put down a series of resolutions, and one of them read, "*Resolved*, To live with all my might, while I do live."[30] His whole life was a commentary on this trite, laconic, fervent, totally honest declaration.

What made Edwards a tragic hero was this ruthlessly intelligent search for the meaning of Puritanism, pursued without regard to the cost. That terrible time in 1750, when his congregation dismissed him, was prefigured in all Edwards had thought and written since he entered Yale in 1716, a precocious young man of thirteen. From the beginning, he had loved God, and taken God's sovereignty seriously. He studied Newton and Locke, with hungry appetite, as he studied theology and apologetics, for the sake of God: "More convinced than ever of the usefulness of free, religious conversation," he wrote into his diary in 1724, deliberately merging an inferior with a superior sphere of inquiry. "I find by conversing on Natural Philosophy, that I gain knowledge abundantly faster, and see the reasons of things much more clearly than in private study: wherefore, earnestly to seek, at all times, for religious conversation."[31] He was

---

[30] *Resolutions*, in *Works*, I, 4.
[31] *Diary*, February 6, 1724. *Works*, I, 12.

never the self-sufficient philosopher, always the strenuous servant of a higher power; he was aware, he wrote, that he was "unable to do anything without God." And, aware of that, he resolved with characteristic energy, "To endeavour to obtain for myself as much happiness, in the other world, as I possibly can, with all the power, might, vigour, and vehemence, yea violence, I am capable of, or can bring myself to exert, in any way that can be thought of."[32] This devout violence marks all his work, even the most scholarly, and it led inescapably to that day, July 1, 1750, when Edwards preached his farewell sermon to a congregation that had voted to do without him—without *him*, Jonathan Edwards, the grandson and successor of Solomon Stoddard, who had for many years ruled western Massachusetts, they said, like a Protestant Pope.

It was an inescapable day because Jonathan Edwards insisted on rescuing the essence of the Puritan faith, on clarifying it, defending it, and preaching it to an age that did not wish to listen. Apologists for Edwards have made light of his most notorious performance, the Enfield sermon of 1741; at Enfield, Edwards had sent his hearers into fits of moaning, weeping, and lamentations by portraying man, with horrible specificity, as a sinner in the hands of an angry God, held over the flaming pit of hell by a thin thread, like a spider or other loathsome insect. It is true that this was not all of Edwards. He was as

---

[32] *Resolution* No. 22, not in *Works*; printed in Clarence H. Faust and Thomas H. Johnson, eds., *Jonathan Edwards, Representative Selections* (1935), p. 39.

much the scholar and the polemicist as he was the fisher of souls. And often, he preached not hell fire for the damned but, with lyrical conviction, blissful peace for the saved. His doctrine of God satisfied his need to humble himself, to feel himself a vile worm before pure and ineffable Power, but it also satisfied his vigorous aesthetic appetite: his conviction of God's sovereignty, he said, was a "delightful conviction" which appeared to him "very often" as "exceeding pleasant, bright, and sweet."[33] That, after all, as we know, was a central theme in his projected history of redemption: it would display God's design as "most beautiful and entertaining," musical in its "admirable contexture and harmony."[34] All this is true. But to minimize the importance, and explain away the doctrine, of the Enfield sermon is to do Edwards a dubious favor; it is to make him inoffensive by emasculating him. Edwards did not want to be inoffensive. God was omnipotent, God was angry, man was wholly lost without God: these were the pillars sustaining the structure of Edwards' theology. To dissolve them into metaphors or disguise them with quibbles and qualifications would be to play Satan's game.

The central importance of these teachings to Edwards is plain: he reiterated them often enough. He reminded himself of them over and over again in his resolutions and his private notebooks. He expounded them in Boston, in 1731, in a sermon reminding his hearers that God should

---

[33] *Personal Narrative, Works,* I, 15.
[34] See above, p. 91.

be glorified in his work of redemption, and that man greatly depended on the Lord; the sermon was, significantly, Edwards' first public success.[35] He insisted upon them in his major writings, his psychological, apologetic, and metaphysical treatises: appropriately, his last book, *The Great Christian Doctrine of Original Sin Defended*, which was in the press when he died, was a refusal to make theology palatable or pretty. And he drew the last consequences of his teachings, bluntly and fatally, for his own congregation: for years, Edwards had followed his grandfather's practice of admitting to communion all who made their profession of faith, and who deserved admission by a sober walk of life. But then, in the 1740's, after the fervor of the Great Awakening, which seemed to promise an enlargement of the churches with pure, converted new members, Edwards changed his mind; gradually, first obliquely and privately, then openly, he sought to restore the primitive Puritan practice of admitting only visible saints, to revive the religious aristocracy of the heroic age of Bradford and Winthrop. Reluctantly but, once certain, without hesitation, Edwards contradicted Solomon Stoddard, and reversed his own practice. It was folly, and Edwards, knowing it was folly, preached it, convinced that he must testify to the truth as he had come to see it. He was asking his Puritan

---

[35] The importance of this sermon has often been singled out; notably by Herbert W. Schneider, *The Puritan Mind* (1930), pp. 103-104; and Perry Miller, *Jonathan Edwards* (1949), pp. 3-40.

congregation to accept the burden of its Puritan past, and it wrecked his career.

III

Edwards' tragedy was personal, but it was not wholly private. It participated in, and, with its poignant protagonist, illuminates a larger tragedy: the failure of the Puritan errand in America. From the days of Bradford and Winthrop down to Edwards' day, and with ever increasing acuteness, the American Puritans faced a dilemma from which there was no escape, the dilemma that besets all Utopians unfortunate enough to secure power. While the welcome confusions and complexities of their life often saved them from the agony of making clear-cut and irrevocable decisions, the American Puritans had at bottom two choices, and both threatened them with disastrous consequences. They could continue to idealize, and seek to perpetuate, the temper of the Founding Fathers; or they could try to adapt themselves to drastic changes in political, economic, and intellectual conditions. Rigid, they would turn themselves into anachronisms; flexible, they would betray their Puritanism.

This dilemma arose only because the Puritans made such high demands on themselves. Puritan theology was crisis theology, but no civilization—especially no prosperous civilization—can long sustain the tension of continuous crisis. As the founders died, as the threats of starvation and disease, treacherous Indians and persecuting Anglicans receded, the routine of living and of doing business invaded the noble dream of a religious refuge set apart from the world as a hiding place and a model. The world, this world, loomed larger than it should for a pilgrim, whose true home is heaven. The great crusade collapsed while, and largely because, New England flourished.

It was a cruel and ironic fate. The American Puritans had suffered the trauma of separation from a cherished landscape; the first generation above all suffered in addition from the guilt of their disobedience: no amount of political sophistry or theological dialectic could wholly numb their awareness that they had defied, and were continuing to defy, established authorities in church and state. That is why the early American Puritans were even more rigid, even more conservative, than other Puritans in easier circumstances; that is why they clung to a few certainties that time could not touch, above all to their ideal of a religious community that was nothing more than a large family. The social thought of the early Puritans in America was essentially the Puritan family ideal—hierarchical, disciplinarian, homogeneous, soberly affectionate and earnestly dedicated to a religious purpose —projected upon society as a whole. But later generations discovered that the sheer passage of time, and new circumstances, made this social ideal unenforceable, reactionary, irrelevant. Thus the American Puritans lost mastery over their society as they lost control over their families.

This loss was troublesome enough, but the Puritan dilemma lay deeper still, concealed in the very nature of Puritan piety. Like other Christian churches, Puritans had many grounds for their belief, offered many reasons for its validity. They cared nothing for the sanctity of tradition, the authority of priesthood, or the miraculous efficacy of ritual—these superstitious innovations they left to the Papists. Instead, they appealed to the authority of a sacred book, the ineffable power of the divine person, the mystical certainty induced by private experience. As dialecticians and lovers of learning, they also appealed to the rational persuasions of logic, and to the scientific and aesthetic coherence of the natural order, but these were inferior, if important and satisfying arguments. They recognized man as a rational creature, and admired him as made in God's image, but they emphasized his sin, his estrangement from his divine father, and the dimming of his reason after the Fall. In consequence, they could be deft logicians, cultivated theologians, and competent scientists: the glacial age of American Puritanism was not an age of obscurantism, Philistinism, or superstition. But their emphasis on the divine sovereignty and on human depravity led them to confine the new philosophy—the physics of Newton and the epistemology of Locke—to a clearly marked and distinctly subordinate sphere. The Arminians, for their part, with their optimistic view of human nature, their prideful account of the capacity of human reason to penetrate the meaning of the universe, could adopt the new philosophy with little loss of theological rigor. A good Arminian could be a good Newtonian with no inner stress. But the Puritans could not permit the scientific world view to penetrate their style of thinking, although they could utilize the practical results of science to heal the sick, satisfy natural curiosity, or confirm God's glorious skill. Increasingly as time went on, there were modern Christians among the New England Congregationalists—Jonathan Edwards deplored their influence in his sermons on the Work of Redemption—but these preachers, men like Charles Chauncy or Jonathan Mayhew, paid a price for their modernity: they surrendered the citadel of their Puritan faith.

The burden of Edwards' work was a protest against this surrender. He was anything but an obscurantist, and, in his feverish intellectual excitement over the ideas of Newton and Locke, he sought to express the old religion in new ways. But the results were, as they had to be, pathetic: Jonathan Edwards philosophized in a cage that his fathers had built and that he unwittingly reinforced. The religious implications of Locke's sensationalist philosophy were inescapable, and they were drawn with surprising unanimity by Locke himself, by Locke's many followers, and by his detractors: revelation, to be true revelation, can be nothing more than an extension of reason; nearly all religious doctrine is either redundant or superstitious. For Locke, the only dogma a Christian need believe—the only dogma he can believe—is that Christ is the Messiah. But Edwards went right on accepting the testimony of Scriptures as literally true, accepting the predictions of the Apocalypse as authoritative history. He read Locke in careful isolation: Locke's psychology gave him useful material for understanding the quality of religious emotion, but little else.

Edwards' reading of Newton was equally parochial. It led him into some ingenious speculations about the nature of the physical universe and the future of mankind. Newton himself, it is true, was not a Newtonian all the time; unlike Locke, he left it to others to explicate, and to complete, his system; unlike Locke, he found pleasure in delving into Biblical chronology and chiliastic prophecies. But, whatever Newton's private religious explorations— and they remain a matter of heated controversy—the ultimate religious direction of Newton's system was away from fundamentalism, away from chiliasm—away, in a word, from Puritanism—toward rationalism, Unitarianism, simple Theism. The physical universe of Edwards was not the physical universe of Newton: it was a universe created in six days, filled with angels and devils, with a heaven and a hell, a universe in the hands, and at the mercy, of an angry God. Edwards did not become a Puritan, or remain a Puritan, as a result of his philosophical and scientific inquiries; he exploited modern ideas and modern rhetoric to confirm religious convictions he had held all his life, and accepted on other grounds.

The complete incompatibility of Edwards' system of ideas with the new world of enlightened philosophy has been obscured by Edwards' vocabulary. It is not that he adopted modish words for modish purposes; but he delighted in intellectual investigation, his ear was sensitive, and his curiosity acute. Hence he felt the power of the new imagery and the new language, and freely used them in his writings. He appealed to "history, observation, and experience," and claimed, as a good empiricist, to bow to fact. But the history he cited was the infallible Scriptures; the observations he noted are the observations of Biblical characters or contemporary Christians in a state of religious trance; the experience he valued was the revelation that gives man knowledge of God. Edwards' facts are of the same order.[36] The *Essay Concerning Human Understanding* and the *Principia Mathematica* may have been important to him, the Pentateuch and the book of Revelation were indispensable. "A great Divine," Ezra Stiles justly called Edwards, "a good linguist" and "a good Scholar," thoroughly versed in "the Logic of Ramus and Burgersdisius, & the philosophy of Wendeline," but not in "the Mathematics & the Ratiocina of the Newtonian Philosophy."[37]

Edwards' spiritual isolation was exacerbated by his physical isolation.[38] In Europe, the ideas of Newton and Locke called forth vigorous debate; they were tested and extended. The followers of Newton and Locke, goaded by their critics, gradually constructed an enlightened intellectual system of great power and lasting influence. Edwards had no such advantages; when he corresponded

[36] I owe this illustration to Vincent Tomas' critique of Perry Miller's *Jonathan Edwards*; see "The Modernity of Jonathan Edwards," *New England Quarterly*, XXV (1952), 60-84, esp. 75-82.

[37] Diary entry, May 24, 1779; "Presidents of Colleges with whom I have been personally acquainted." Quoted in Ola Elizabeth Winslow, *Jonathan Edwards, 1703-1758* (1940; reprinted 1961), p. 337.

[38] See Edwards' letter to Edward Wigglesworth, the liberal professor of Divinity at Harvard, written in 1757: "I can't assign any particular acquaintance as my warrant for troubling you with these lines; not being one of them that have been favored with opportunities for such an advantage." Quoted in Johnson, "Edwards' Background of Reading," p. 196.

with Europeans, it was mainly with like-minded clerics; when he read—and he read deeply and voraciously—he read mainly books that would feed his Puritan convictions, or books that he thought he needed to refute. The outside world existed mainly to supply him with echoes. Far from being the first modern American, therefore, he was the last medieval American—at least among the intellectuals.

IV

Every tragedy has its irony, and the tragedy of Jonathan Edwards is no exception. The world, Edwards wrote in his sermons on the redemption, would soon come to an end; the time of the millennium and the apocalypse was not far away. But the world, it seemed, went on, more worldly than ever before. Americans, to be sure, continued to worship the old God, and even advanced clergymen welcomed the evangelical invasion of Whitefield—at least for a while. But the old God wore new, almost unrecognizable guises; his yoke was easy, and his burden light. And Americans turned to new guides in the writing of history, discarding Providence, and seeking the causes of events within the natural realm. The best history the Puritans could write was written by Thomas Prince, a diligent compiler, a discriminating book-collector, a patient chronicler, but little more. It was to be other historians, rationalists like Governor Thomas Hutchinson, who were to rejoin the main stream of the European intellect. When Edwards' *History of the Work of Redemption* was finally published in 1774, the *Monthly*

Review spoke for prevailing opinion, both in Old England and New, in a contemptuous notice. Far from being new, the reviewer noted, the book was "a long, laboured, dull, confused rhapsody," the revival of a medieval method that should have been buried long since: "It is merely an attempt to revive the old mystical divinity that distracted the last age with pious conundrums: and which, having, long ago, emigrated to America, we have no reason to wish should ever be imported back again." The book is visionary, presumptuous, reactionary, extravagant, a species of "pious nonsense" spouted by a "poor departed enthusiast."[39] There could be no question: the world went on. Yet, in an ironic sense, Edwards' chiliastic prediction was fulfilled, and in his lifetime. Only it was Jonathan Edwards' world, and with it the world of Puritanism, that came to an end.

---

[39] *The Monthly Review; or, Literary Journal*, LII (January to June, 1775), 117-120.

Bibliographical Essay

Bibliographical Essay

The conception that has guided my judgment of the Puritan historians is the distinction between critical and mythical thinking. Critical thinking is disenchanted thinking; in holding nothing sacred, it moves freely through every subject and asks questions of all; it ranges from the crudest positivism to the most refined intellectual inquiry. Mythical thinking, on the other hand, is incapable of this sort of penetration; at a low level, it is animistic and superstitious; at its highest level, it allegorizes and sublimates but retains at least a shred of the miraculous—of that which must remain untouched by profane hands. This distinction, it is worth admitting, is a value judgment: I regard critical thinking as essentially superior to mythical thinking, no matter how lovely the myth or elegant the allegory. It follows that I consider history based on critical thinking superior to history based on myth, and Puritan history was at heart mythic. To say this is not to say that religious men cannot write good, even great history: the example of Ranke would instantly refute this assertion. Indeed, an atheist can write bad history as easily as a Christian can. But as long as myth pervades the historian's mind, there are areas in which he will be unhistorical—*which* area depends, of course, on his myth.

Obviously, the historian must handle the distinction between myth and criticism delicately, with discretion;

in judging the performance of past historians, he is himself likely to be limited in his objectivity by his ideology or his character. But he is free to judge his peers: history is a discipline with its own criteria of excellence; it is public, self-corrective, never complete, and in this sense, scientific. And in its character of science, history is a progressive discipline—that is to say, a discipline capable of progress as well as regression. I repeat: religious men, devout Christians, have written great histories, and have made significant contributions to the techniques of history—in Bradford's century one thinks of Mabillon and the Benedictines of St. Maur, or of the Bollandists. Yet even these masters were shackled by their piety: they could be scrupulous, accurate, inventive, scientific only within a certain framework. It was reserved to secular historians—in antiquity, in the Renaissance, in the Enlightenment, and in the professional atmosphere of the nineteenth and twentieth centuries—to push history toward full scientific status.

But history, in addition to being a science, is also an art, and Christian historians have written imperishable works of historical art. That is why my judgment of William Bradford is so favorable, my judgment of Cotton Mather so severe. That is why my judgment of Jonathan Edwards, in whom art and science were in irreconcilable conflict, is complex.

While the distinction between criticism and myth is not new—it goes back to Goethe and Heine—it has been made most persuasively and most learnedly in our own day by Ernst Cassirer, above all in *The Philosophy of Symbolic Forms*, 3 vols. (1923, 1925, 1929; transl. by Ralph Manheim, 1953, 1955, 1957). Cassirer has expounded his views also in shorter form, especially in *Language and Myth* (1925; transl. by Suzanne K. Langer, 1946). I refer the reader to my *The Enlightenment: An*

Interpretation, Volume I, *The Rise of Modern Paganism* (1966), where I have celebrated the work of Cassirer, and of his associates at the Warburg Institute—Erwin Panofsky, Fritz Saxl, and others—in detail, and worked out the meaning of critical thinking for the Enlightenment. The ideas of the Warburg group, which have received only limited attention in this country, could be immensely valuable to American historians.

One. THE STRUGGLE FOR THE CHRISTIAN PAST

Moriz Ritter's long article, "Die christlich-mittelalterliche Geschichtsschreibung," *Historische Zeitschrift*, CVII (1911), 237-305, ably outlines the problems of Christian historiography. Walther Lammers has collected a useful group of German articles on medieval historiography, *Geschichtsdenken und Geschichtsbild im Mittelalter* (1961); while a number of these were published in the Nazi period, they are generally free from the vicious nonsense that disfigured the scholarship of those historians who chose to remain, and remain active, in the Hitler *Reich*. Marc Bloch's masterly *Feudal Society*, 2 vols. (1939-1940; transl. by L. A. Manyon, 1961), has some perceptive pages on medieval modes of historical thinking (I, 72-75, 88-92). See also V. H. Galbraith, *Historical Research in Medieval England* (1951) which, though hardly exciting, is reliable. Friedrich Heer, *The Medieval World: Europe, 1100-1350* (1961; transl. by Janet Sondheimer, 1962), has a good chapter (XI) on the writing of history. I found a long recent study by H. Fuhrmann, "Die Fälschungen im Mittelalter," *Historische Zeitschrift*, CXCVII (1963), 529-554, and his answers to critics, *ibid.*, 580-601, highly interesting; it shows how vulnerable medieval man was to forgeries. Among medieval histories, perhaps the most important are the books by Otto of Freising: *The Two Cities*, C. C. Mierow, ed. and transl. (1928), and *The Deeds of Frederick Barbarossa*, ed. Mierow (1953). My own thinking on Christian historiography and on Cassirer's distinction between critical and mythical thinking has been clarified by the remarkable books of Erich Auerbach. Auerbach's magnificent survey of realism in literature, *Mimesis: The Representation of Reality in Western Literature* (1946; transl. by Willard R. Trask, 1953), should be read in conjunction with *Scenes from the Drama of European Literature: Six Essays* (various dates; transl. by Ralph Manheim and Catherine Garvin, 1959), which contains the essay "Figura," a penetrating account of "figural thinking" in the Christian millennium; see also Auerbach's posthumous *Literary Language and Its Public in Late Latin Antiquity* (1958; transl. by Ralph Manheim, 1965). Like Ernst Cassirer, Erich Auerbach has much to say to the American historian.

Christian historiography is often called, a little loosely, Augustinian; it is a usage I have employed too, though rather sparingly. For all the importance of Augustine's historical writings, they deserve more attention than they have had. H. I. Marrou, *Saint Augustin et la fin de la culture antique*, 4th ed. (1958) is basic; Etienne Gilson, *The Christian Philosophy of Saint Augustine* (1931; transl. by L. E. M. Lynch, 1960) offers a useful general survey. See also Ernst Bernheim's stimulating *Mittelalterliche Zeitanschauungen in ihrem Einfluss auf Politik und Geschichtsschreibung* (1918). M. C. d'Arcy and others have compiled an interesting if often rather popular series of essays, *Saint Augustine* (1930), which has a good deal to say on Augustine's "Christian Humanism" (a doubtful term), and something on the *City of God*. R. Reitzenstein's article, "Augustin als antiker und als mittelalterlicher Mensch," *Vorträge der Bibliothek Warburg 1922-1923* (1924), pp. 24-65, is important. So is Theodor E. Mommsen, "St. Augustine and the Christian Idea of Progress," *Journal of the History of Ideas*, XII (1951), 346-374. In an equally important essay, Mommsen has established that Orosius was quite as prominent a founder of medieval history as Augustine; see his "Orosius and Augustine," in Mommsen, *Medieval and Renaissance Studies*, ed. Eugene F. Rice, Jr. (1959), pp. 325-348. Since few serious historians take eschatology seriously, Karl Löwith's discriminating essay, *Meaning in History* (1949), in which the Augustinian vision of history is central, is a useful corrective to the secular view. See also Ernst Troeltsch, *Augustin, die christliche Antike und das Mittelalter* (1915).

While Burckhardt, the master of all Renaissance historians, did little with Renaissance historiography, the neo-Burckhardtians have extended his fundamental ideas to include it. The writings of Hans Baron are of special significance here; see his general essay, "Das Erwachen des historischen Denkens im Humanismus des Quattrocento," *Historische Zeitschrift*, CXLVII (1933), 5-20; and his masterly work, *The Crisis of the Early Italian Renaissance: Civic Humanism and Republican Liberty in an Age of Classicism and Tyranny*, 2nd ed. (1966), on the "civic humanism" of such Florentine Humanists and historians as Leonardo Bruni. Baron had traced many of his major themes in a splendid essay on the revival of the ideal of the active life (and, implicitly, a critical view of the world) in "Cicero and the Roman Civic Spirit in the Middle Ages and the Early Renaissance," *Bulletin of the John Rylands Library*, XXII (1938). Myron P. Gilmore has two revealing articles, "The Renaissance Conception of the Lessons of History" and "Individualism in

Renaissance Historians," in his collection, *Humanists and Jurists* (1963). Felix Gilbert has written several pioneering essays on the political thought of the great Florentines; his *Machiavelli and Guicciardini: Politics and History in Sixteenth Century Florence* (1965) deals superbly with two masters; one can only wish (how often can one say this?) that the book had been longer. Eugenio Garin, *Der Italienische Humanismus* (transl. from the manuscript by Giuseppe Zamboni, 1947) is not centrally concerned with the historians, but is full of insights. So are the writings of Paul Oskar Kristeller, who deals mainly with the philosophers; see, in addition to several collection of essays, his informative *The Classics and Renaissance Thought* (1955). Wallace K. Ferguson's helpful monograph, *The Renaissance in Historical Thought; Five Centuries of Interpretation* (1948) begins with the Renaissance; Ferguson touches on the same subject in his "Humanist Views of the Renaissance," *American Historical Review*, XLV (1939), 1-28. August Buck, *Das Geschichtsdenken der Renaissance* (1957) is an economical essay, up to date in scholarship but with no surprises. Rudolf von Albertini, *Das florentinische Staatsbewusstsein im Übergang von der Republik zum Prinzipat* (1955) has some good sections on historians, and relates historical writing to political thinking.

For full documentation of my own view that there was one Renaissance, and that it took place in the Renaissance, see my *The Enlightenment*, Volume I, chapter V, and the relevant section of the Bibliographical Essay. Here I mention only Federico Chabod's masterly survey, comprehensive and judicious, "The Concept of the Renaissance," in *Machiavelli and the Renaissance* (transl. by David Moore, 1958). Ernst Cassirer examines the inner tensions of Renaissance thought, the struggle and uneasy truce between mythical and critical thinking, in his *The Individual and the Cosmos in Renaissance Philosophy* (1927; transl. by Mario Domandi, 1963). Significantly, Cassirer's profound book was first published in the series of studies for which the Warburg Institute is justly celebrated: it is for the Renaissance that the work of Aby Warburg and his associates has been of particular significance. The writings of Aby Warburg, the founder, have been conveniently collected in *Gesammelte Schriften*, 2 vols. (1932); they contain his discussion of the Renaissance "compromise formula," the Humanists' attempt to rescue Christian thought while rehabilitating classical thought—a formula of decisive importance for our understanding of Renaissance historical writing. Fritz Saxl, a distinguished member of the Warburg group, has a set of articles collected in *Lectures*, 2 vols. (1957). Erwin Panofsky, perhaps the best known and most prolific member of the Warburg circle, has had great influence among art historians; he should have equally great influence on intellectual historians. Some of his most characteristic shorter articles have been conveniently collected in *Meaning in the Visual Arts* (1955); his *Studies in Iconology: Humanistic Themes in the Art of the Renaissance* (1939) brilliantly traces the rise of a new conception of the world by a close examination of works of art; finally, Panofsky's *Renaissance and Renascences in Western Art* (1960) surveys the modern controversy over the Renaissance, and settles the matter—to my complete satisfaction, in any event—in neo-Burckhardtian fashion.

The rise of the new history on the Continent has been sketched in some highly satisfactory articles. I am indebted to G. Wylie Sypher, "La Popelinière's *Histoire de France*," *Journal of the History of Ideas*, XXIV (1963), 41-54; and to Sypher, "Similarities between the

Scientific and Historical Revolutions at the End of the Renaissance," *ibid.*, XXVI (1965), 353-368. Donald R. Kelley, *"Historia Integra*: François Baudouin and his Conception of History," *ibid.*, XXV (1964), 35-57, is exceptionally rich in insight. Jean Bodin, the great theoretician of history, has been appreciated in a pointed study by Julian H. Franklin, *Jean Bodin and the Sixteenth-Century Revolution in the Methodology of Law and History* (1963). See also Beatrice Reynolds' edition of Bodin's *Method for the Easy Comprehension of History* (1945), and Henri Sée, "La philosophie d'histoire de Jean Bodin," *Revue historique*, CLXXV (1935), 497-505. Leonard F. Dean has traced "Bodin's *Methodus* in England before 1625," *Studies in Philology*, XXXIX (1942), 160-166; we need more such studies of the cosmopolitan influence of historical writings in that cosmopolitan age. For Augustinianism in Renaissance Europe, see Paul O. Kristeller, "Augustine and the Renaissance," *International Science*, I (1941), 7-14; for Augustinianism in France, see the fascinating monograph by William J. Bouwsma, *Concordia Mundi: The Career and Thought of Guillaume Postel (1510-1581)* (1957). History in early modern Germany has been well treated in Paul Joachimsen, *Geschichtsauffassung und Geschichtsschreibung in Deutschland unter dem Einfluss des Humanismus* (1910), and in the more recent book by Emil Clemens Scherer, *Geschichte und Kirchengeschichte an den deutschen Universitäten: Ihre Anfänge im Zeitalter des Humanismus und ihre Ausbildung zu selbständigen Disciplinen* (1927), of which part I is most relevant here. Adalbert Klempt, *Die Säkularisierung der universalhistorischen Auffassung: Zum Wandel des Geschichtsdenkens im 16. und 17. Jahrhundert* (1960), has interesting material on the secularization of historical thinking, mainly in Germany.

Historiography in England both before the rise and during the reign of Puritanism has recently received much attention. C. L. Kingsford, *English Historical Literature in the Fifteenth Century* (1913) (which, despite its title moves at the end into the sixteenth century) may now be supplemented by Denys Hay, *Polydore Vergil: Renaissance Historian and Man of Letters* (1952), which, though brief, is thorough; and by F. Smith Fussner, *The Historical Revolution: English Historical Writing and Thought 1580-1640* (1962), a comprehensive survey of resources open to historians, styles of history, and antiquarianism; it has separate chapters on the major writers —Camden, Raleigh, Stow, Selden, Bacon. Though very useful, Fussner's book has been justly criticized for failing to take into account the powerful impact of the classics on early modern historiography, and for isolating his figures from the Continent in an age when such isolation did not exist. Fussner's judgments, however, are often shrewd—see his appraisal of Raleigh as a survival of medieval, rather than a pioneer of modern, historiography. Christopher Hill, for his part, has sought to prove Raleigh and other Puritan historians modern in his stimulating but exasperating *Intellectual Origins of the English Revolution* (1965). I find the book wrong-headed, as did H. R. Trevor-Roper in an accurate and devastating review essay in *History and Theory*, V (1966), 61-82, a model of informative polemicizing. The older essay by Sir Charles Firth, "Sir Walter Raleigh's History of the World," *Proceedings of the British Academy*, VIII (1919), 427-446, has not lost its uses, but should be supplemented by E. Strathmann, "The History of the World and Raleigh's Scepticism," *Huntington Library Quarterly*, III (1940), 265-287. The best essay on Bacon's histories I know is by Leonard F. Dean, "Sir Francis Bacon's Theory of Civil History-Writing," *English Literary History*, VIII

(1941), 161-183. On English antiquarianism, see T. D. Kendrick, *British Antiquity* (1950), which concentrates on the sixteenth century. While there is material on Camden and Selden, both deserve full-fledged monographs.

I am considerably indebted to two fascinating studies of Shakespeare's history plays, both exceedingly revealing of the cultural atmosphere in Elizabethan England: E. M. W. Tillyard, *Shakespeare's History Plays* (1944), and (if anything even more fascinating than Tillyard's book) Lily B. Campbell, *Shakespeare's 'Histories': Mirrors of Elizabethan Policy* (1947). The place of Machiavelli in English political and historical thinking has been satisfyingly reexamined by the late Felix Raab: *The English Face of Machiavelli: A Changing Interpretation, 1500-1700* (1964). For Puritan historical writing in Elizabethan England, see Norman Sykes, *Old Priest and New Presbyter* (1956), especially pp. 11, 20, 24, for the combat over history between Anglicans and Puritans; these pages show that the appeal to history was by no means the only appeal, and that both sides sometimes even disdained the past for the sake of a claim to some timeless insight into Christian truth. Eleanor Rosenberg, *Leicester, Patron of Letters* (1955) has an excellent chapter (III) on Puritan historians. Finally, William Haller's *The Elect Nation: The Meaning and Relevance of Foxe's 'Book of Martyrs'* (1963) is a magnificent analysis which goes far beyond its announced subject to illuminate Christian historiography as a whole. The book may be supplemented by Haller's own article, "John Foxe and the Puritan Revolution," in Richard Foster Jones *et al.*, *The Seventeenth Century* (1951), pp. 209-224.

Appendix: The word "innovation" was a term of abuse that everyone employed. I shall offer only a handful of instances here. In 1641, the House of Commons explicitly indicted Laud for his ecclesiastical "innovations" (B. H. G. Wormald, *Clarendon: Politics, Historiography and Religion*, 2nd ed. [1964], p. 2). Earlier, at the end of the sixteenth century, archbishop John Whitgift had denounced the Puritans for the same sin: "You cannot be the Queenes friends that thus looke for innouations in the state" (Perry Miller, *Orthodoxy in Massachusetts* [1933], p. 30). In New England, too, this was a favorite word. In 1669, the members of the new Third Church in Boston addressed a memorial to the Governor and Council of the Colony, claiming that they had been traduced by their enemies, and that they were "withoutt any desire of innovation" (Hamilton A. Hill, *Old South Church* [see below, p. 139], p. 51). In 1699, when the new Brattle Street church had been formed (see above, p. 86), Cotton Mather confided to his diary: "I see *Satan* beginning a terrible Shake unto the Churches of *New England*; and the *Innovators*, that have sett up a *new Church* in *Boston*, (a new one indeed!) have made a *Day of Temptation* among us." And again, a few days later, Cotton Mather determined to testify "against the *Innovations*, that are going to shake our churches." (*Diary*, I, 329, 331.)

Two. WILLIAM BRADFORD: CAESAR IN THE WILDERNESS

For this chapter, as for all chapters, this bibliographical essay does not aim at completeness; it is a personal essay. Nor is it necessary to be exhaustive: the annotated bibliographies (revised by George McCandlish) appended to the second edition of Perry Miller and Thomas H. Johnson, eds., *The Puritans: A Sourcebook of their Writings*, 2 vols. (1963), are more than adequate.

The strange history of William Bradford's manuscript
has been told several times; best by Samuel Eliot Morison's "Introduction" (pp. xxvii-xl) to his edition of
Bradford's *Of Plymouth Plantation, 1620-1647* (1952).
Morison also conveniently lists all the editions. Morison's
own edition, as he himself puts it (p. vii), is "modern
(*not* modernized)" and it makes splendid reading. It has
only one flaw: it distorts the leisurely pace, and characteristic seventeenth-century manner, of Bradford's history by pulling out many of the letters and other documents and grouping them together in appendices; this
gives the book a deceptively modern speed. The best
edition, which I have used here, archaic spelling and all,
is by Worthington C. Ford, 2 vols. (1912). It retains the
spelling everywhere, including the running heads, but
then inconsistently modernizes the title: "Of Plymouth
Plantation." An insignificant fault; the annotations and
illustrations are superb.

Bradford Smith's biography, *Bradford of Plymouth*
(1951), has been widely praised, by Morison among others, but it is often vulgar, and resorts a little desperately
to imaginary conversations and ill-founded conjectures.
While Smith's biography is not useless, I prefer the short
appreciative life of Bradford by Samuel Eliot Morison in
the *Dictionary of American Biography*, and Morison's
biographical remarks in his "Introduction" to Bradford's
Of Plymouth Plantation. This "Introduction" also contains a list of Bradford's other writings and their fate. In
preparing my chapter on Bradford, I have studied these
writings, including the "Letter Book," *Collections of the
Massachusetts Historical Society*, first series, III (1794),
27-76; "Description and Historical Account of New
England in Verse, from a MS.," *ibid.*, first series, III
(1794), 77-84; two poems: "Of Boston in New England,"

and "A Word to New England," *ibid.*, third series, VII (1838), 27-28; "A Dialogue or the sume of a Conference between som younge men borne in New England and sundery Ancient men that came out of holland and old England anno dom. 1648," *Publications of the Colonial Society of Massachusetts*, XXX (1920), 115-141; "Governor Bradford's Dialogue between Old Men and Young Men, Concerning 'The Church and the Government thereof,' " *Massachusetts Historical Society Proceedings*, XI (1870), 396-482. There are several Bradford letters reprinted in *The American Historical Review*, VIII (1902-1903), 294-301; and in *Collections of the Massachusetts Historical Society*, fourth series, VI (1863), 156-161. Bradford's *Mourt's Relation* (with Edward Winslow) was first printed in 1622; it is available in Edward Arber, ed., *The Story of the Pilgrim Fathers, 1606-1623 A.D.* (1897), pp. 395-505 (this early work, as my colleague Alden Vaughan has pointed out to me, is rather brighter in tone than Bradford's later masterpiece).

For Bradford's style—for his use of alliteration, inversion, metaphor, and other devices—see the comprehensive and reliable article by E. F. Bradford: "Conscious Art in Bradford's *History of Plymouth Plantation*," *New England Quarterly*, I (1928), 133-157. Much earlier, Moses Coit Tyler had appreciated Bradford both as a writer and as a historian in his pioneering *A History of American Literature, 1607-1765* (1878; reprinted 1962), pp. 123-130. Other histories of American history begin with Bradford and have some good pages on him: see J. Franklin Jameson's short but penetrating sketch, *The History of Historical Writing in America* (1891); and Michael Kraus, *The Writing of American History* (1953), which surveys the field with brevity and intelligence. See also Kenneth B. Murdock, *Literature and Theology in Colo-*

nial New England (1949), especially chapter III; Murdock, "Clio in the Wilderness: History and Biography in Puritan New England," *Church History*, XXIV (1955), 221-238; and Richard S. Dunn, "Seventeenth-Century English Historians of America," in James Morton Smith, ed., *Seventeenth-Century America* (1959), pp. 195-225. All three are general surveys of high caliber and I have learned from them all; all three give Bradford his due, briefly. Since New England Puritans, historians and others, were much influenced by the sermon, a book like W. Fraser Mitchell, *English Pulpit Oratory from Andrewes to Tillotson* (1932) is indispensable.

Bradford, as I make clear in the text, found himself compelled to write contemporary history. For the Humanists' view of that branch of historical writing, see the fine pages in Felix Gilbert, *Machiavelli and Guicciardini*, pp. 205-207, and the persuasive brief argument offered in behalf of contemporary history by H. Stuart Hughes in "Is Contemporary History Real History?" (*History as Art and as Science* [1964], pp. 89-107). As for Bradford's bias, as I suggest in the text (see above, p. 42), discriminating as most students of Bradford may be, they are perhaps all too favorably inclined to him, and even credulous. Hence the skepticism of Charles McLean Andrews, especially in his *The Colonial Period of American History*, Volume I (1934), is welcome.

For the English background of the American Puritans the literature is exceedingly rich. George F. Willison, *Saints and Strangers* (1945), superficial but generally accurate and informative, takes the pilgrims from England to Holland to Plymouth. Andrews, just cited, and Herbert L. Osgood, *The American Colonies in the Seventeenth Century*, particularly Volume I (1904), see the Imperial background clearly. (For the controversy between the American exceptionalists and the Imperial historians, consult the interesting intellectual biography, *Charles McLean Andrews: A Study in American Historical Writing* [1956], by A. S. Eisenstadt.) Andrews has some pertinent questions concerning the "persecution" of Puritans in "Historic Doubts Regarding Early Massachusetts History," *Publications of the Colonial Society of Massachusetts*, XXVIII (1935), 280-294. For English Puritanism, William Haller, *The Rise of Puritanism* (1938), and Haller, *Liberty and Reformation in the Puritan Revolution* (1955), are both indispensable; they are based on superb knowledge of all the sources, particularly the Puritan sermons. M. M. Knappen's generous survey, *Tudor Puritanism: A Chapter in the History of Idealism* (1939), begins with the English Reformation, follows the Marian Exiles and their return to England; the second part on the intellectual and social ideas of the English Puritans is valuable, as is the long bibliographical essay on "the historiography of Puritanism" (pp. 494-518). Leonard J. Trinterud, "The Origins of Puritanism," *Church History*, XX (1951), 37-57, traces the heritage of Puritanism back to medieval English piety. A general study of the English Reformation, brilliantly informed and judicious, is A. G. Dickens, *The English Reformation* (1964), a splendid book. For Cambridge, the cradle of so many Puritan intellectuals, there are two good books, one by H. C. Porter, *Reformation and Reaction in Tudor Cambridge* (1958), the other by Mark H. Curtis, *Oxford and Cambridge in Transition, 1558-1642* (1959). Christopher Hill may be partisan, but is often illuminating; his collection of articles, *Puritanism and Revolution: The English Revolution of the Seventeenth Century* (1958) has much good material; though his best book remains *Economic Problems of the Church From Archbishop*

Whitgift to the Long Parliament (1956), where his own political stance works to his advantage. For the politics of Elizabethan England, J. E. Neale's *The Elizabethan House of Commons* (1949), and Neale, *Elizabeth I and her Parliaments, 1559-1601*, 2 vols. (1953, 1957), are simply indispensable; Neale's collection, *Essays in Elizabethan History* (1958), contains much that is of value. For general histories, the two volumes in the Oxford History of England, J. B. Black, *The Reign of Elizabeth*, 2nd ed. (1959), and Godfrey Davies, *The Early Stuarts, 1603-1660*, 2nd ed. (1959), are both satisfactory. J. E. Neale, *Queen Elizabeth* (1934) is popularization at its best. A. L. Rowse's flamboyant volumes on Elizabethan England have sold exceedingly well, and do not lack insight, but they are marred by vulgarity and a certain imitation Elizabethan gusto that makes them useless on the Puritans. Let me add only two other books: H. R. Trevor-Roper's vigorous, highly secular *Archbishop Laud*, 2nd ed. (1962), which seeks to reevaluate a controversial figure; and A. S. P. Woodhouse, ed., *Puritanism and Liberty*, 2nd ed. (1951), which contains the Leveler debates and tracts, and a splendid "Introduction," characterizing the divisions among the Puritans.

The Dutch interlude of Bradford and his fellow-Pilgrims is important for more than biographical reasons: here the rigid English Calvinists first encountered the relaxed theology of Arminianism and participated in the quarrels between Dutch Orthodoxy and Dutch Dissent. See the relevant chapters of Bradford Smith, *Bradford of Plymouth*, and Willison's chapters in *Saints and Strangers*; but these should be supplemented by Henry Martyn Dexter, *The England and Holland of the Pilgrims* (1905), and, above all, by D. Plooij, *The Pilgrim Fathers from a Dutch Point of View* (1932), both of which are the result of excellent research; see also, Raymond P. Stearns, *Congregationalism in the Dutch Netherlands* (1940). Douglas Nobbs, *Theocracy and Toleration: A study of the Disputes in Dutch Calvinism from 1600 to 1650* (1938); A. W. Harrison, *The Beginnings of Arminianism to the Synod of Dort* (1926); and the fine economical study by R. L. Colie, *Light and Enlightenment: A Study of the Cambridge Platonists and the Dutch Arminians* (1957), together give a comprehensive picture of what the Pilgrims faced in Holland—and would later face in New England.

As for New England: the transmission of European, especially English, cultural patterns to the new world is the leading theme of most books devoted to seventeenth-century America. One of the most successful of these is Sumner Chilton Powell, *Puritan Village: The Formation of a New England Town* (1963), a model analysis of cultural migration: detailed and discriminating. At the other end of the scale is Daniel J. Boorstin, *The Americans: The Colonial Experience* (1958), in many ways informative, but designed in general to establish the independence of Americans from—and their superiority to—European "ideas." Two recent editions of seventeenth-century documents provide exceptional insights into the Puritan mind in America: Bernard Bailyn, ed., *The Apologia of Robert Keayne: The Self-Portrait of a Puritan Merchant* (1964); and Edmund S. Morgan, ed., *The Diary of Michael Wigglesworth, 1653-1657: The Conscience of a Puritan* (1946). Samuel Eliot Morison, *Builders of the Bay Colony*, rev. ed. (1964), and Morison, *The Intellectual Life of Colonial New England* (1956; this is the second revised edition of a book first published under the title, *The Puritan Pronaos* [1936]), were both extremely helpful to me; in conjunction with Thomas Goddard Wright's dependable survey, *Literary Culture in Early New England, 1620-1730* (1920), a book to which Morison refers in appreciation, these volumes present a believable portrait of Puritan life in the first century here. Morison's institutional histories are filled with pertinent information and written with Morison's customary zest: I am indebted to *The Founding of Harvard College* (1935), and *Harvard College in the Seventeenth Century*, 2 vols. (1936).

Morison's volumes are, of course, part of the great campaign of rehabilitation that had been going on since the 1920's. The history of Puritan historiography in this country is a long and fascinating drama. The Puritans themselves supplied much information about their life here, and while Bradford's masterpiece was not published in full until 1856, the manuscript had been available to many historians, both in the seventeenth and eighteenth centuries. By the time that Cotton Mather published his *Magnalia Christi Americana* in 1702, Puritan history was well (and favorably) known, and entered into the mainstream of American mythology—to the degree that citations seemed no longer necessary. (Samuel Eliot Morison is surely right to denounce George Willison's lament of "neglect" as "nonsense": all the "essential parts of the Pilgrim story," Morison writes ["Introduction," Bradford's *Of Plymouth Plantation*, pp. xxx-xxxi], "had been in print since 1669"; and indeed, "all eighteenth-century historians of the English colonies mention the Plymouth Colony in its right place and give it the proper emphasis." And what is true of Plymouth is equally true of the Massachusetts Bay Colony.) The best eighteenth-century history of Massachusetts, Governor Thomas Hutchinson's *History of the Colony of Massachusetts-Bay* (1764-1828; best edition by Lawrence Shaw Mayo, 3 vols. [1936], supplemented by Catherine Barton Mayo's "Additions to

Bibliographical Essay

Thomas Hutchinson's *History of Massachusetts-Bay,*" *Proceedings of the American Antiquarian Society*, LIX [1949], 13-74), was certainly well known. The Puritans haunted American men of letters as much as they occupied historians and ancestor-worshipers—as the poems of Longfellow and the stories of Hawthorne make clear with painful clarity. While ladies, goaded by the stream of immigrants from Eastern and Southern Europe, organized the Daughters of the American Revolution (significantly enough in 1890), students of history and literature continued to study the Puritans, and indeed with a new freedom, in sharp contrast to the snobbish ancestor-worship around them. Moses Coit Tyler, in his *History of American Literature, 1607-1765*, which had appeared in 1878, discovered a large number of minor American writers, but wrote of them with care and without unction; local historians published reliable documents (it was in these years that the activity of the Massachusetts Historical Society reached impressive heights). Perhaps the best local history (it is a book that I used with great profit) was a parochial history, Hamilton Andrews Hill's copiously documented *History of the Old South Church (Third Church), Boston, 1669-1884*, 2 vols. (1890). It was in the same period that serious self-criticism began, and it began in an unimpeachable quarter—in the Adams family. "Least of all," Perry Miller was to write many years later in some astonishment, could the Puritans "have believed that perhaps the greatest mind to be born of all the orthodoxy's numerous progeny, a lineal descendant of stalwart Peter Bulkley of Concord, would survey their handiwork and denominate the era inaugurated by the *Cambridge Platform* not that of 'ye good way,' but that of an 'intellectual glacier'" (*Orthodoxy in Massachusetts, 1630-1650* [1933], p. 313). That phrase about the glacier stung, and has retained its sting; I know of no epithet that has been repeated more often, either with approval or disapproval, than this. It was coined by Charles Francis Adams, Jr., in a pair of lectures delivered of all places at Harvard, and later published in a provocative little volume, *Massachusetts: Its Historians and Its History* (1895). With sovereign contempt for the relativistic philosophy of historicism, convinced that there must be one law, one judgment, for all civilizations, Adams condemned what he considered the hypocrisy, the cruelty, the hostility to life of his Puritan forefathers, and delineated an intellectual decline which excepted only Cotton Mather's *Magnalia* from its sweep. It was after the Antinomians had been banished, and John Cotton had died, that there settled over New England a "theological glacier," and in consequence, for a hundred and fifty years "absolutely nothing" of any value was produced (pp. 59, 67). In the Preface to his *Intellectual Life of Colonial New England*, Samuel Eliot Morison takes vehement exception to this judgment, and other historians have devoted learned articles or even volumes to proving it false. (The best of these, I think, is Clifford K. Shipton, "The New England Clergy of the 'Glacial Age,'" *Publications of the Colonial Society of Massachusetts*, XXXII [1937], 24-54.) As readers of this book will remember, I have, despite all this modern criticism, adopted Adams' phrase (see above, p. 25), though, as I trust my book makes clear, I do not give it the full weight that Adams gave it; I explicitly suggest that "glacier" refers to neither superstition nor stupidity, but a tragic failure to keep up with intellectual developments in Europe.

Three years before he published his lectures, Charles Francis Adams had already published a fine survey of the social history of the Bay Colony (*Three Episodes of Mas-*

sachusetts History, 2 vols. [1892]), which remains valuable, and a few years before that, in 1887, his brother Brooks had launched a full-scale assault on the Puritans in *The Emancipation of Massachusetts*. While the Daughters of the American Revolution continued to celebrate their ancestors, and some exceptional scholars (like Barrett Wendell; see below, p. 146) lamented the new critics, for a time the critics held the upper hand. In 1921, James Truslow Adams restated the critics' case in his persuasive, smoothly written account of the first century of Massachusetts and its neighbors in *The Founding of New England*, which secured wide popularity and, significantly enough, the Pulitzer Prize for History. The case against the Puritans was strengthened by the mad interlude of Prohibition which its most articulate opponents, notably H. L. Mencken, placed squarely on the shoulders of New England Congregationalists. Mencken derided the Puritan as a thin, dour, hypocritical enemy to all pleasure; in Mencken, Puritans—all Puritans—sweat a great deal, and expend their best efforts, their most devoted vigilance, preventing everyone from enjoying himself. This protest of thirsty Americans was reinforced by Progressives who detested the Puritans as the source of all that was reactionary in the politics of the Harding-Coolidge millennium. V. L. Parrington's influential *Main Currents in American Thought*, Volume I, *The Colonial Mind, 1620-1800* (1927), contrasted two types, liberals and Puritans, and portrayed the Puritans as oligarchic, theocratic, harsh, and reactionary. Parrington's political and literary views are no longer so influential as they once were—they have been mercilessly attacked for their dogmatism, their crudity, their ignorance, never more effectively than in Lionel Trilling's splendid dissection, "Reality in America," in *The Liberal Imagination: Essays on Literature and Soci-*

ety (1951), pp. 3-21. But for many years Parrington had the authority that the Adams brothers had enjoyed half a century before.

The Adams-Mencken-Parrington interpretation of Puritanism gradually loosened its hold on American readers—partly with Repeal; partly with the political experience of the thirties and forties which taught, if it taught anything, the need for a certain discrimination and caution in the use of labels; and partly with the rebellion of respectable scholars. From the 1920's on, while Mencken was making his witticisms, a handful of scholars, mainly at Harvard, set out to revise and indeed unthrone the dominant interpretation. Barrett Wendell had died in 1921, but his work was carried on by George L. Kittredge (see below, p. 147); by Kenneth B. Murdock, whose *Increase Mather, The Foremost American Puritan* appeared in 1925 (see below, p. 147); by Samuel Eliot Morison, whose vigorous style and sound scholarship won many converts to the side of the revisionists; and above all by Perry Miller, the historian who, more than any other, penetrated the recesses of the Puritan mind.

Without doubt, Perry Miller was a great historian. He has often been accused of being unnecessarily difficult, and I think it is true that Miller liked to puzzle his readers by using involuted sentences, or by telling his story incompletely. It is also true that his writing often lacks refinement: his Puritans "shriek," his Puritans are rarely concerned, always "tormented," Cotton Mather's lust for publication is "monstrous," and so forth. These twin flaws of Miller's style, his intermittent failure to communicate (one of my friends, an American historian, has called Miller's *The New England Mind: The Seventeenth Century* an "autistic performance") and his overwriting, are linked to what I regard as a somewhat eccentric interpretation of the American Puritans: he makes them (and especially their ideas) more important, more philosophical, than in fact they were. In his "Introduction" to the anthology, *The Puritans*, which he edited with Thomas H. Johnson (see above, p. 131), an Introduction which may be the best thing Miller ever wrote on the Puritans—it courageously tackles all the pressing issues, and makes some subtle distinctions—Miller speaks of "Puritan Humanism"; and indeed, he liked to portray the American Puritans as the heirs of Erasmus, as highly trained logicians in the school of Ramus. As I think I have shown in this book, these high claims cannot be sustained.

I have one other criticism of Miller's work—apart from my reservations about his book on Jonathan Edwards (see below, pp. 154-155): it is Miller's somewhat undiscriminating fertility. Miller had so many ideas that practically every interpretation one can think of finds its place in his pages. Now clearly there is good reason for complexity: Cotton Mather, say, was both a pedant and more than a pedant, the American Puritans both accepted and rejected elements of the European Renaissance. But Miller often embraced distinct and incompatible interpretations without showing the dialectical tension that would make them both credible (for an instance of this, his interpretation of the Jeremiads, see below, p. 150).

But having said this, I return to it: Miller was a great historian. He read most of what the Puritans wrote, and he knew much about their European background. As a proclaimed atheist, he was of course in an impregnable position to celebrate the Puritans: it was demonstrably an act of supreme historical detachment (Perry Miller's strategic position was thus the exact counterpart of the Adams' position: no one could accuse Brooks Adams or Charles Francis Adams of deriding the Puritans out of envy). In his great trilogy, *Orthodoxy in Massachusetts, 1630-1650; The New England Mind: The Seventeenth Century* (1939), his most original but also his most opaque book; and *The New England Mind: From Colony to Province* (1953), which is I think his greatest work and an authentic masterpiece; in a series of essays (conveniently collected in *Errand Into the Wilderness* [1956]) and anthologies (like *The Puritans*, which has been deservedly influential, and *Roger Williams: His Contribution to the American Tradition* [1953], which rescued Williams from Parrington's naive praise of him as a modern religious liberal), Perry Miller has built up a complex canvas; he has shown that most of his predecessors, admirers and detractors of Puritans alike, had really not taken the trouble to study Puritanism in America with sufficient care (although Miller's debt to Charles Francis Adams, I think, has not been adequately appreciated). In consequence, every student of American Puritanism must begin with Miller, even if he does not end with him. (While it is perhaps too early to assess his work with finality—the tributes collected in *The Harvard Review*, II, No. 2 [1964], are touching and revealing but hardly conclusive—I am certain that Perry Miller's place in the history of American history will remain a prominent one.)

Since Miller's day, the best work on the American Puritans has been on significant aspects of social and economic history, and this work extends, refines, and to some degree modifies Miller's general interpretation without seriously damaging it. I have learned much from Bernard Bailyn, *The New England Merchants in the Seventeenth Century* (1955), and Bailyn's long essay, followed by an illuminating bibliography, *Education in the Forming of American Society* (1960), both splendid examples of the new social history. I am also much indebted to Edmund S. Morgan's perceptive *The Puritan Family: Religion and Domestic Relations in Seventeenth-Century New England* (1944; 2nd. ed., 1966), as well as Morgan's *Visible Saints: The History of a Puritan Idea* (1963), which helps to clarify a complicated principle of Puritan church organization. Morgan has also written a persuasive biography of John Winthrop, *The Puritan Dilemma* (1958), which throws light not merely on the plight of the religious Utopian in an imperfect world, but which was of special use to me in my studies of Winthrop the historian. (Winthrop's Journal, called "History of New England," has been well edited by James Kendall Hosmer, 2 vols. [1908]. A full analysis of Winthrop's "History" is much needed.) Other recent monographs of value include Larzer Ziff, *The Career of John Cotton: Puritanism and the American Experience* (1962), an excellent attempt to clarify the career of an elusive, indeed devious, Puritan; Emery Battis, *Saints and Sectaries: Anne Hutchinson and the Antinomian Controversy in the Massachusetts Bay Colony* (1962), an interesting essay, using modern techniques to understand a vexed case; Darrett B. Rutman, *Winthrop's Boston: Portrait of a Puritan Town, 1630-1649* (1965), an intelligent, but to my mind not wholly successful, attempt to interpret the early Massachusetts experience as a failure in Utopianism—despite my problems with the thesis, I have learned much from the book. As I look at this recent scholarship—especially the writings of Bailyn and Morgan—I discern the direction that post-Miller scholarship is likely to take: analytical rather than synthetic, a stress on social and economic themes relatively slighted by Miller, a careful modification of some of Miller's views and choice *among* some of his contradictory views, and, finally, a reexamination of the

Europeanness of the early American experience. It is to this last aspect of post-Miller scholarship that I trust the present book is a contribution.

Three. COTTON MATHER: A PATHETIC PLUTARCH

Cotton Mather wrote a great deal. For good bibliographical indications, see Thomas H. Holmes, *Cotton Mather: A Bibliography of His Works*, 3 vols. (1940), and J. L. Sibley's biography in his *Biographical Sketches of Graduates at Harvard University*, Volume III (1885), 42-158. Kenneth B. Murdock's *Selections* (1926), conveniently available in paperback (1960), contains a useful selected list of Mather's writings (pp. lxi-lxii). Mather's diaries, which he carefully edited, have been published: *Diary of Cotton Mather*, ed. Worthington C. Ford, 2 vols. (1911-1912); the missing diary of 1712 has recently been unearthed and edited by William R. Manierre, II (1964). It is to be hoped that the promised edition of the *Magnalia Christi Americana*, to be edited by Kenneth Murdock *et al.*, will appear soon. The leading biography of Cotton Mather is by Barrett Wendell, *Cotton Mather, The Puritan Priest* (1891; ed. 1963 with a long apologetic introduction by Alan Heimert). Wendell's sympathetic biography was more useful in his day, when the diaries, from which it draws, were unpublished, than in ours, when the diaries are available. It is useful to have someone favorable to Cotton Mather write his life—so many have disliked him so intensely—but the final verdict strikes me as unconvincing, despite Heimert's defense. Still, I accept Wendell's contention that Mather, far from being exceptional, was "a conveniently exaggerated type of the characteristics that marked the society of which he formed a part." What holds true of Wendell's biography of the son holds true of Kenneth Murdock's biography of the father: it is good to have, but its judgment should not be taken without reserve. The best short appraisal of Cotton Mather's character and reputation that I have seen is David Levin, "The Hazing of Cotton Mather: The Creation of a Biographical Personality," *New England Quarterly*, XXXVI (1963), 147-171. Levin makes the interesting point that even historians sympathetic to American Puritans (like Samuel Eliot Morison) are willing to sacrifice Cotton Mather to the anti-Puritans, the better to show their objectivity. Levin proves that much of the abuse Cotton Mather has had to take from later historians rests on shaky evidence, often maliciously interpreted, but Levin's own rather favorable estimate of Mather strikes me as just as speculative. Perry Miller's pages on him in *New England Mind: From Colony to Province* are extremely suggestive, and I am much indebted to them.

For Mather and witchcraft, see the last chapter of George L. Kittredge, *Witchcraft in Old and New England* (1929); and the much older William F. Poole, "Cotton Mather and Salem Witchcraft," *North American Review*, CVIII (1869), 337-397, which both seek to exculpate Cotton Mather; Perry Miller's relevant pages in *From Colony to Province* take an original and convincing line. Mather the scientist has been the subject of much apologetic literature, notably by George L. Kittredge. See his "Cotton Mather's Election into the Royal Society," *Publications of the Colonial Society of Massachusetts*, XIV (1913), 81-114; and "Cotton Mather's Scientific Communications to the Royal Society," *American Antiquarian Society Proceedings*, XXVI (1916), 18-57, which together clarify a tangled affair and establish Mather's right to call himself F.R.S. On the controversy over inoculation, see Kittredge, "Some Lost Works of Cotton

Mather," *Massachusetts Historical Society, Proceedings,* XLV (1912), 418-479; but also, John B. Blake's informative "The Inoculation Controversy in Boston: 1721-1722," *New England Quarterly,* XXV (1952), 489-506, which takes a judicious and rather cool look at the role of the Mathers, father and son, in the affair. Otho H. Beall, Jr. and Richard H. Shryock have published parts of Cotton Mather's medical treatise, "Angel of Bethesda," with pertinent comments: *Cotton Mather: First Significant Figure in American Medicine* (1954). Other relevant items are listed in the magnificent bibliography in Miller and Johnson, *The Puritans,* mentioned before. What emerges, once the parochialism and apologetics have been cleared away, is Cotton Mather the civilized but cautious Christian, feeling his way in a world changing under his hands.

On Mather the stylist, I am with the minority. Moses Coit Tyler, Barrett Wendell, and Kenneth Murdock all profess to find Cotton Mather a good writer: Murdock, to strengthen his case, quotes Wendell: "The style, in the first place, seems to me remarkably good . . . "; in the whole *Magnalia,* Wendell writes, "I have not found a line that is not perfectly lucid, nor many paragraphs that, considering the frequent dulness of his subject, I could honestly call tiresome." (This judgment appears in Wendell's *Cotton Mather,* and is reproduced, generally with approval and only minor amendments, in Murdock's *Selections* from Cotton Mather, p. xxxix.) As a reader of the *Magnalia,* I dissent. I find myself in rather close agreement with Howard Mumford Jones in his survey, "American Prose Style: 1700-1770," *Huntington Library Bulletin,* No. 6 (1934), 115-151. For Mather as a biographer, note the favorable verdict of Samuel Eliot Morison that he, for one, found Mather's life of John

Eliot "more useful than any other biography of the Apostle" to the Indians (*Builders of the Bay Colony*, rev. ed. [1964], p. 394). It is certain that Cotton Mather diligently searched records that have since been lost; hence his documents are invaluable. It has become fashionable to impute to the Puritans a special passion and capacity for biography—Kenneth Murdock is particularly insistent on this point (see his "Clio in the Wilderness" [cited above, p. 134]). But the argument is purely deductive: since the Puritans were compelled by their faith to practice severe introspection, and since they were anxious to find in their activities possible signs of grace, they had a special vocation for history (which is public biography), biography (which is private history), and the journal (which is the raw material for both). The record will not bear out this deduction. Anglicans, Lutherans, Roman Catholics, and unbelievers loved history, wrote biographies, and kept journals quite as much as the Puritans did. See especially Donald A. Stauffer, *English Biography Before 1700* (1930), an excellent survey with a helpful bibliography. John A. Garraty's essay, *The Nature of Biography* (1957) is full of useful indications. Further support for my argument that the passion for history was not special to the Puritans can be found in Louis B. Wright, *Middle Class Culture in Elizabethan England* (1935).

For historians of Mather's generation see the fine pages in Tyler, Murdock, and Dunn. See also, Kenneth B. Murdock, "William Hubbard and the Providential Interpretation of History," *Proceedings of the American Antiquarian Society*, LII (1942), 15-37. Hubbard's *Narrative* has been edited by S. G. Drake under the title, *The History of the Indian Wars in New England* (1865). Hubbard's *A General History of New England, From the Discovery to MDCLXXX* was first printed in *Collections of the Massachusetts Historical Society*, second series, V-VI (1815). Perry Miller's conjecture (*From Colony to Province*, p. 136) that the history was suppressed because it displeased "certain elements," though plausible, must remain conjecture. The best edition of Increase Mather's *Brief History of the War with the Indians in New-England* is by S. G. Drake (1862). The passage from this book that I have quoted in the text (above, p. 56) has also been noticed by Michael Kraus, *The Writing of American History* (1953), p. 31. On the literature about the Indian wars, which aroused much vigorous writing, see Samuel Eliot Morison's felicitous summary, *The Intellectual Life of Colonial New England*, pp. 183-194. These histories are set into historical perspective in Alden T. Vaughan's excellent monograph, *New England Frontier: Puritans and Indians, 1620-1675* (1965).

The seminal work on the second-generation Puritans, on New England in transition, is Perry Miller's *New England Mind: From Colony to Province*. It contains, among many other good things, the classic analysis of the sermon as Jeremiad (a term first used, to my knowledge, by Charles Francis Adams). But, fertile as it is, Miller's analysis of the Jeremiad suffers from that indecisiveness to which I have referred before: Miller describes the Jeremiad both as a cleansing ritual unconnected with any real belief that New England was in fact decaying, and as a factual declaration, deeply pessimistic. Its meaning depended on the man who pronounced it, and on the time at which it was pronounced, but Miller does not make this clear. Bailyn's *New England Merchants* and Morgan's *Puritan Family* (above, pp. 144-145) are indispensable. There is a revealing discussion of late seventeenth-century politics (a neglected subject) in Richard S. Dunn, *Puritans and Yankees: The Winthrop Dynasty of New*

England, 1630-1717 (1962), which might well become a model for further studies. Carl Bridenbaugh discusses an equally neglected subject in his *Mitre and Sceptre: Transatlantic Faiths, Ideas, Personalities, and Politics, 1689-1775* (1962), which deals with Anglicanism in America—another chapter in the unity of Western civilization. Bridenbaugh's *Cities in the Wilderness: The First Century of Urban Life in America, 1625-1742* (1938) includes rich materials on Boston in transition. I found the opening two chapters of George Sensabaugh, *Milton in Early America* (1964) an important discussion of the cultivation of colonial America.

The claim that the American Puritans were the heirs of the best that Renaissance Europe had to offer has become part of our historical folklore; hence Alan Simpson's comment is important: "Professor Morison's determination to make humanists out of his Puritans appears in *Harvard College in the Seventeenth Century*," and his other books. "The success of his efforts may be judged from Professor Miller's compliment: 'Thanks to the labors of Professor Morison, we may now rest assured that the Puritans of New England were the disciples of Erasmus and Colet.' . . . The problem is one of emphasis, but the end of all education in early New England is best stated simply as in E. S. Morgan's chapter on 'The Education of a Saint,' in *The Puritan Family* . . . : 'The main business of education was to prepare children for conversion.' " (Simpson, *Puritanism in Old and New England* [1955], p. 118.) Needless to say, I am with Morgan—and with Simpson, whose lucid, independent interpretation of the great Puritan crusade, which went bankrupt in the end, is among the best things on Puritanism that I have seen.

For changes in historical thinking in Europe in the time

of Cotton Mather, see the splendid essays by David Knowles on the Bollandists and the Benedictines in his *Great Historical Enterprises* (1963). See also David Douglas, *English Scholars: 1660-1730*, 2nd. ed. (1951), a model of a monograph. Leonard Krieger, *The Politics of Discretion: Pufendorf and the Acceptance of Natural Law* (1965), has a helpful chapter (VI) on Pufendorf as historian. For liberal English theology in this time, see the old but by no means dated work by John Tulloch, *Rational Theology and Christian Philosophy in England in the Seventeenth Century*, 2 vols. (1872). It may now be supplemented by Ernst Cassirer's perceptive monograph, *The Platonic Renaissance in England* (1932; transl. by James P. Pettegrove, 1953); by J. A. Passmore, *Ralph Cudworth: An Interpretation* (1951); by Olive M. Griffiths, *Religion and Learning: A Study in English Presbyterian Thought from 1662 to the Foundation of the Unitarian Movement* (1935); by H. John McLachlan, *Socinianism in Seventeenth-Century England* (1951); and by G. R. Cragg, *From Puritanism to the Age of Reason: A Study of Changes in Religious Thought Within the Church of England, 1660 to 1700* (1950)—all excellent.

The relation of the Glorious Revolution to the events in New England is only beginning to be explored; see Dunn and Bridenbaugh (above, pp. 150-151), and Michael G. Hall *et al.*, eds., *The Glorious Revolution in America: Documents on the Colonial Crisis of 1689* (1964). The classic works on colonial history by Andrews and Osgood are not dated. See, finally, G. R. Cragg, *Puritanism in the Period of the Great Persecution, 1660-1688* (1957), which deals with a period, and with events, to which the ruling circles in Boston were exceedingly sensitive.

Bibliographical Essay

Four. Jonathan Edwards: An American Tragedy

As I trust I have made clear in the text, I have considered Jonathan Edwards as a historian, not as a theologian, and, while I regard his historical work as a great failure, I insist on his stature. It is for this reason that I have used the much-abused word "tragedy" to describe his fate.[1]

The writings of Jonathan Edwards have been collected several times, and the editions are related to one another in rather confusing ways (see the bibliographical indications in *Jonathan Edwards, Selections*, Clarence H. Faust and Thomas H. Johnson, eds. [1935; rev. ed., 1962], pp. cxix-cxxi). I have used the four-volume edition of 1857, a reprint of the Worcester edition. Unfortunately the edition that will doubtless be definitive—the Yale edition begun under the general editorship of Perry Miller—has so far only reached the second volume: Volume I, *Freedom of the Will*, ed. Paul Ramsay (1957), and Volume II, *Religious Affections*, ed. John E. Smith (1959). Both offer scrupulous versions of the text, and are equipped with full scholarly, if sometimes a little adulatory, introductions. Ola Elizabeth Winslow, *Jonathan Edwards, 1703-1758* (1940; reprinted 1961) is a sound though rather pedestrian biography; it has a good bibliographical essay which lists a number of unpublished materials (pp. 339-361). The edition of *Selections*, just cited, is excep-

---

[1] In seeking guidance on the appropriate use of the word "tragedy," I have relied particularly on the following expositions: F. L. Lucas, *Tragedy, Serious Drama in Relation to Aristotle's 'Poetics,'* 2nd ed. (1962); Oscar Mandel, A *Definition of Tragedy* (1961); Gilbert Norwood, *Greek Tragedy* (1960); and H. D. F. Kitto, *Greek Tragedy: A Literary Study*, 3rd ed. (1954). Auerbach, *Mimesis, passim*, is decisive on the absence of tragedy in Christianity.

tionally full and intelligent in its choices; it has a long introduction and a splendidly annotated bibliography.

The best known and most controversial biography is by Perry Miller: *Jonathan Edwards* (1949); it has been praised and damned, but it has left no one indifferent. Certain facts are beyond dispute: the book is a skillful combination of biography and interpretation; it is inconvenient to use, for it has no footnotes and the most skimpy bibliography; it is badly overwritten, overloaded with such muscular terms as "momentous," "immense," and "awful." Its thesis (which Miller maintains throughout the book including the climactic last chapter which is significantly on history) is that Edwards was the most remarkable, the most original of colonial thinkers, and not only that: that he was supremely modern, the first, perhaps the only colonial to take Newton and Locke seriously, and to develop their ideas into a startling modern system that would have done an Einstein or Freud proud. This thesis is, in a word, absurd. Miller propounds it by trying to overwhelm the reader with his confident formulations, his weighty asides, his emphatic rhetoric, and large and unprovable claims.[2] As my readers know, my own view of Edwards as a historian is the very opposite of Miller's; much as I admire Perry Miller as a historian, and much as I have learned from him, his *Edwards* strikes me as simply perverse. Among all the reviews of the book I have seen, the long, devastating, and to my mind superb analysis by Vincent Tomas, "The Modernity of Jonathan Edwards," *New England Quarterly*, XXV (1952), 60-84, is by far the most persuasive. See also the review by

---

[2] In 1948 Perry Miller repeated his claims for Edwards' modernity in his edition of some unpublished notes of Edwards: *Images or Shadows of Divine Things* (1948).

Joseph Haroutunian in *Theology Today*, VII (1951), 554-556.

For the vast array of comment on Edwards, see the bibliographical essay in Faust and Johnson (cited above, p. 153). Here I list only a selection of useful articles. Thomas H. Johnson, "Jonathan Edwards' Background of Reading," *Publications of the Colonial Society of Massachusetts*, XXVIII (1931), 193-222, discusses in revealing detail just what Edwards read in the course of his life. (Incidentally, there is a passage in Miller's *Edwards* which puzzled me from the beginning: "In 1739 he gave a series of sermons on the idea [of redemption.] Thereafter, the journals show, he read with avidity every historical work he could lay his hands on, and made long lists of others he hoped to read" [pp. 307-308]. But, as I suggest in the text [see above, pp. 92-94], his later writings show no evidence of acquaintance with the major historical writings then being published in Europe. I consulted Professor Thomas A. Schafer of the McCormick Theological Seminary; according to Professor Schafer, Edwards' historical interest continued unabated, and his notebooks show continuing concern with the history of redemption, but his reading seems to have been mainly in the book of Revelation, and in Ezekiel. According to Professor Schafer, the modern historians he seems to have read most actively were such ecclesiastical historians as Fleury, Lampe, and Thomas Mott. Edwards' lists include very little secular history, and not one of the great historians of the day—Robertson or Hume or Voltaire—are so much as hinted at. Professor Schafer's illuminating letters to me suggest that further study of Edwards' historical notebooks would repay close attention; but it seems highly unlikely that they would yield much evidence of Edwards' interest in profane history.) Clarence H.

Faust, "Jonathan Edwards as a Scientist," *American Literature*, I (1930), 393-404, disposes of the sentimental legend that Edwards was, or might have become, a great scientist. C. C. Goen has some discriminating observations on "Jonathan Edwards: A New Departure in Eschatology," *Church History*, XXVIII (1959), 25-40; Joseph Haroutunian's "Jonathan Edwards: a Study in Godliness," *Journal of Religion*, XI (1931), 400-419; and Haroutunian, "Jonathan Edwards: Theologian of the Great Commandment," *Theology Today*, I (1944), 361-377, are two sympathetic and comprehending attempts to understand Edwards' thought as a whole. I found Herbert W. Schneider's chapter (IV) on Edwards in his *The Puritan Mind* (1930) especially illuminating; it covers the range of Edwards' thought in brief space. H. Richard Niebuhr, *The Kingdom of God in America* (1937), has some brilliant pages on Edwards' eschatology. Clyde A. Holbrook, "Jonathan Edwards and His Detractors," *Theology Today*, X (1953), 384-396, was useful to me: I found in it the reference to the brutal review in *The Monthly Review* of 1775 which I quote in the text (see p. 117). Vincent Buranelli, "Colonial Philosophy," *William and Mary Quarterly*, third series, XVI (1959), 343-362, is comprehensive, and finds a prominent place for Edwards.

There are some good books on Edwards' world. Robert J. Taylor, *Western Massachusetts in the Revolution* (1954) analyzes the politics of Edwards' dismissal from his Northampton pulpit. Leonard J. Trinterud studies *The Forming of an American Tradition: A Re-examination of Colonial Presbyterianism* (1939), which was a formidable rival to Edwards' Congregationalism. Joseph Haroutunian's *Piety Versus Moralism: The Passing of the New England Theology* (1932) traces the decay of the kind of piety of which Edwards was among the last representatives. Conrad Wright gives generous space to Edwards in his fine analysis of *The Beginnings of Unitarianism in America* (1955), while Edwin Scott Gaustad offers an intelligent if concise sociological analysis of *The Great Awakening in New England* (1957), in which Edwards had such a prominent part. I learned much from Richard M. Gummere, *The American Colonial Mind and the Classical Tradition: Essays in Comparative Culture* (1963), a collection of informative articles on the classical learning of colonial Americans. Robert Middlekauff's *Ancients and Axioms: Secondary Education in Eighteenth-Century New England* (1963) is also very helpful. For eighteenth-century historiography in America before the Revolution, see the relevant chapter in Kraus (cited above, p. 133); and the useful article by Stow Persons, "The Cyclical Theory of History in Eighteenth Century America," *American Quarterly*, VI (1954), 147-163. H. Trevor Colbourn, *The Lamp of Experience: Whig History and the Intellectual Origins of the American Revolution* (1965) has much good material on the growth of a Whig interpretation of history in early eighteenth-century America, but suffers from a certain lack of cross-cultural references: Colbourn tends to take as meaningful declarations about the craft of history the time-honored clichés that readers of Cicero had been repeating for centuries.

Index

theme of decay and loss, 50; reflection of nostalgia and fear in *Of Plimmoth Plantation*, 50; elegy-like quality of his annals at the end, 52; death of, 53; manuscript of, copied by New England historians, 54; theology of, upheld by Mather's *Magnalia*, 71, 75; story told by, used by Jonathan Edwards, 109, 110

Brattle Street Church, 86

Brattle, William, 86; letter of, to son, 24

Brewster, William, 37

Caesar, comparison of Bradford with, as historian, 43

Calvin: work of, in preaching martyrdom of Christians, 32; Puritan's acceptance of, 80; quoted, 85

Calvinists: admission by, that the Lord tempered justice with mercy, 34; doctrine of, exemplified in work of Jonathan Edwards, 97, 104, 105

Camden, William, 19, 41

Casaubon, Isaac, proof by, of invalidity of Baronius' annals, 21

Charles II, Restoration of, 78

Chaucer, 7

Chauncy, Charles, 113

Christian Philosopher, The (Cotton Mather), 82, 84

Cicero, 17

Clark, Samuel, 64; studied by Cotton Mather, 62; quoted, 63

Classicism and Christianity, 23

Colman, Benjamin, 86

Condillac, Étienne, author of *Essai sur l'origine des connaissances humaines*, which laid foundation for Enlightenment's psychology, 92

Cotton, John, grandfather of Cotton Mather, 74, 75, 77

Cromwell, Oliver, 80

Cushman, Robert, 46

Davenport, John, 73-74

Douglass, William, Dr., medical opposition to smallpox inoculation led by, 83

Edwards, Jonathan: series of sermons by, on the work of redemption, 88; occupation of, for nineteen years, with writing of *History of the Work of Redemption*, 89-91, 93-104; death of, after inoculation for smallpox, 91; Calvinist philosophy of, 104-105; dismissal of, by his congregation, 106; farewell sermon, 107; Enfield sermon, 107-108; first public success of, in 1731 Boston sermon, 109; last book of, *The Great Christian Doctrine of Original Sin Defended*, 109; career wrecked by asking his congregation to accept the burden of its Puritan past, 109-110; incompatibility of Edwards' system of ideas with enlightened philosophy, 114; posthumous publication of